Queering Wolverine in Comics and Fanfiction

Queering Wolverine in Comics and Fanfiction: A Fastball Special interrogates the ways in which the Marvel Comics character Wolverine is a queer hero and examines his representation as an open, vulnerable, and kinship-oriented queer hero in both comics and fanfiction.

Despite claims that Wolverine embodies Reagan-era conservatism or hegemonic hypermasculinity, Wolverine does not conform to gender or sex norms, not only because of his mutant status, but also because his character, throughout his publication history, resists normalization, making him a site for a queer-heroic futurity. Rather than focusing on overt queer representations that have appeared in some comic forms, this book explores the queer representations that have preceded Wolverine's bisexual and gay characterizations and in particular focuses on his porous and vulnerable body. Through important, but not overly analyzed storylines, representations of his open body that is always in process (both visually and narratively), his creation of queer kinships with his fellow mutants, and his eroticized same-sex relationships as depicted in fanfiction, this book traces a queer genealogy of Wolverine.

This book is ideal reading for students and scholars of comics studies, cultural studies, gender studies, sexuality studies, and literature.

Christopher Michael Roman is Professor of English at Kent State University and specializes in Comics Studies and the Graphic Novel, LGBTQ+ Literature, and Queer Theory. His comics studies work has been published in the *Journal of Graphic Novels and Comics* and *IJOCA*. He is also author of *Domestic Mysticism in Margery Kempe and Julian of Norwich* (2005) and *Queering Richard Rolle* (2017). He is the co-editor of the collection *Medieval Futurity* (2021).

Routledge Focus on Gender, Sexuality, and Comics

Series Editor: Frederik Byrn Køhlert, University of East Anglia

Routledge Focus on Gender, Sexuality, and Comics publishes original short-form research in the areas of gender and sexuality studies as they relate to comics cultures past and present. Topics in the series cover printed as well as digital media, mainstream and alternative comics industries, transmedia adaptions, comics consumption, and various comics-associated cultural fields and forms of expression. Gendered and sexual identities are considered as intersectional and always in conversation with issues concerning race, ethnicity, ability, class, age, nationality, and religion.

Books in the series are between 25,000 and 45,000 words and can be single-authored, co-authored, or edited collections. For longer works, the companion series "Routledge Studies in Gender, Sexuality, and Comics" publishes full-length books between 60,000 to 90,000 words.

Series editor Frederik Byrn Køhlert is an associate professor of American Studies at the University of East Anglia. In addition to several journal articles and book chapters on comics, he is the author of *Serial Selves: Identity and Representation in Autobiographical Comics*.

Gender and Sexuality in Israeli Graphic Novels
Matt Reingold

Infertility Comics and Graphic Medicine
Chinmay Murali and Sathyaraj Venkatesan

Queering Wolverine in Comics and Fanfiction
A Fastball Special
Christopher Michael Roman

https://www.routledge.com/Routledge-Focus-on-Gender-Sexuality-and-Comics-Studies/book-series/FGSC

Queering Wolverine in Comics and Fanfiction
A Fastball Special

Christopher Michael Roman

Routledge
Taylor & Francis Group

LONDON AND NEW YORK

First published 2023
by Routledge
4 Park Square, Milton Park, Abingdon, Oxon OX14 4RN

and by Routledge
605 Third Avenue, New York, NY 10158

Routledge is an imprint of the Taylor & Francis Group, an informa business

British Library Cataloguing-in-Publication Data
A catalogue record for this book is available from the British Library

ISBN: 978-1-032-12014-0 (hbk)
ISBN: 978-1-032-12015-7 (pbk)
ISBN: 978-1-003-22264-4 (ebk)

DOI: 10.4324/9781003222644

Typeset in Times New Roman
by codeMantra

Contents

Acknowledgments

This book has been in the works for a few years now, and I am incredibly thankful for all of the people who have been supportive of this project. I would like to first thank my PhD students, Kara Cremonese, Devin Fairchild, William Heade, and Amir Saffar Perez, who inspired me to think deeply about comics, pulps, mutants, and fan studies. It is exciting to know how vibrant and exciting popular culture studies and comic studies will become with talented students like these joining the field. I would also like to thank the graduate students in my Queer Comics Seminar where some of these ideas were tested out: Keragen Corpening, Christine Harles, Brittany Helmich, Mischa Klenovich, Maggie Orosz, Corey Pate, April Sharp, Alex Coleman, Jennifer Hedges, Gabby DiDonato, David Jansen, and Lauren Olesh. These students went along for a queer ride through comics in the middle of a pandemic and managed to make this seminar thought-provoking and fun. I would also like to thank Anna Peppard, J. Andrew Deman, and Chris "Mav" Maverick for having me on their podcast *Oh Gosh Oh Golly Oh Wow* to discuss Wolverine and his queerness. The greater comics studies community is truly welcoming, and I am very happy to have found a place in it. I would also like to thank the larger comics studies community on Twitter. Social media can be a toxic place, but I have been inspired by the comics studies scholars and X-Twitter accounts who care deeply about comics and the X-Men and have led me to sources that I may not have previously known.

This work could not have been completed without a generous Summer Fellowship granted by Kent State University.

As with all my work, the greatest thanks go to my family. To my sons, Jacob and Isaac, who share my love of comics in varying degrees. For the pure joy they give us, I also have to thank Groot (the dog) and Rocket (the cat). Rocket is our newest family addition, and boy, is he a ball of personality. Finally, I could not do what I do without the love and support of my wife, Nicole, who encourages me and challenges me in all the ways that I need.

Introduction

A Fastball Special

Wolverine has gone by many names in his comic book history: Logan, Patch, Wolverine, Weapon X, James Howlett, just to name a few. These names speak not only to how writers and artists have reimagined the character over the years, they also indicate the fluid nature of Wolverine's character. Wolverine is a mutant with a healing factor that allows him to heal from almost any injury and keeps him from aging like normal humans. He also has claws, first bone claws in his youth, then, as an adult, adamantium-laced claws and skeleton after the adamantium-bonding process performed on him while he was kidnapped by the Weapon X program. Wolverine is an enigma. His power is one of healing, self-regeneration, but also destruction; his adamantium claws are his signature characteristic; however, using them causes him great pain. He is both honorable and feral. His body, experimented upon by having it infused with metal, makes him indestructible. Not only did a shadowy government organization try to make him into a weapon, but he has been mind-wiped numerous times so he does not remember his history. As well, his mutant power of healing makes him forget traumatic events. He is always forging ahead, proud to be a member of the X-Men and a mutant. At the same time, he tries to recover his past which has been lost to mind-wipes and his healing factor. He is lost in queer time. The Wolverine is a complicated character with a rich history that spins off in many directions. As this book will explore, he is a hybrid: a cyborg, along with his categorization as a mutant, and as such, he is ostracized by the human community in the Marvel Universe because of his difference.

Yet, this rich history has been unexplored through a queer theory lens, one which unpacks the typical reading of him as a hypermasculine cowboy. Wolverine is one of Marvel's most popular characters, even to the point of fans complaining of Wolverine saturation. In the 1990s and 2000s, for example, Wolverine appeared not only in his own self-titled book, but on a number of teams from the X-Men to the New Avengers with appearances in nearly every title from *Ghost Rider* to the *Fantastic Four*. As Mike Avila comments, "In the early 1990s, he was so popular, he guest-starred in a non-X-Men comic for nearly three consecutive years" (2021: 183). It is because of his ever-present

DOI: 10.4324/9781003222644-1

representation, and the fan reaction that Wolverine induces, that Wolverine is worth examining for his queerness.

An indicator of how fans react to Wolverine can be found in the letter pages of *Wolverine* #50 (1992). Commenting on issue #47, letter writer Joe Christiano comments that the issue was enjoyable because "an entire issue went by, and Wolverine didn't kill a single person! That was amazing" (*Wolverine* #50 1992: 46). Christiano goes on to write "it's nice to change pace once in a while and show the nobler side of him" (*Wolverine* #50 1992: 46). The letter included right after Christiano's letter, written by Richard Holton, comments "I'm a very big fan of the Wolverine comics and didn't appreciate how soft the issue made him look. Wolverine didn't even kill the guy after he was shot" (*Wolverine* #50 1992: 46). While, Christiano celebrates a Wolverine that is more "hesitant to kill," Holton wants his Wolverine to be steeped in blood. Readers like Holton have dominated the discussion of Wolverine, however, seeming to overlook Wolverine's reticence in using his claws. The discrepancy between these two treatments of Wolverine lends itself to a queer reading; Wolverine's very complexity between his berserker nature and his fight for nobility indicates just how non-normative this character can be.

Wolverine's history is rich with queer moments, and he challenges what it means to be masculine through his vulnerability and nurturing of other mutants. My choices for stories to explore have to do with representations of Wolverine not as the hacking killer, but rather where he is shown to be more vulnerable, exhibit mentorship through the care of young mutants, and is queered through visual and narrative representation. As Anna Peppard writes,

> because the Western world's sexual prejudices are deeply intertwined with [...] rejections of the body as a meaningful location of culture or identity, unpacking the sexual possibilities of the superhero body can only enhance the value of that body as an object of study.
>
> (2020: 13)

As I will explore, Wolverine's body is repeatedly a site of queer representation as its hybrid nature suggests something beyond the human-animal binary. His body is rhizomatic, a term coined by Gilles Deleuze and Felix Guattari in which "there is no truth, no single reality, no static beings or essences. There are always many possible truths and realities that all be viewed as social constructs" (Jeffrey 2016: 14). To think of Wolverine as rhizomatic is to acknowledge Wolverine as an assemblage, one constituted by writers, artists, and readers, as well as by the material circumstances of his creation. This book argues that what makes Wolverine queer is his transcendence of normative binaries such as human/animal or masculine/feminine to embody a both/ and construction. He does not fit neatly into categories, and what I call his "too-muchness"—too much hair or too much love—is a queer response to a superhero masculinity that is marked by heteronormativity and wholeness.

This book employs queer theory as a lens to examine Wolverine's representation. Queer theory, however, is not a monolithic theory, so I utilize different tools in the queer toolbox to examine these comics. Queer theory has many different manifestations and many voices contributing to it. Queer theory as an academic study appeared in the 1990s building on the word "queer," formerly a slur, and later recovered in the 1980s and used as a term for non-normative subjectivities and identity. Queer was further utilized in activist circles during the rise of HIV/AIDS. Activism, in the form of groups such as ACT-UP, had a profound influence on the theory part of queer theory as it challenged the shaming of queer bodies and argued for the liberation of queer identity while pushing back against the stigma of HIV/AIDS found in politically conservative circles. Queer theory, as a term, was coined by Teresa de Lauretis in 1990 as a way to transcend codified gay and lesbian identities. Queer theory, in essence, questions normative gender and sexual identities and resists fixed categories of gender and sexuality such as sex and gender binaries (male/female, masculine/feminine). It calls into question normativity, broadly defined as norms propagated by heteronormative institutions and thought (such as traditional concepts of marriage). Many scholars employ "queer" as a verb meaning to question the object of study's normality; this is the strategy I employ in this book. Queer can also work as an identity which challenges not only heterosexual identity but also LGBT identities that have become normalized (also called homonormativity). Though veering in many different directions, queer theory's foundational goals are showing how gender and sexuality is both constructed and performed.

The queer theory I employ in this book examines Wolverine's non-normativity. As I will discuss below, many critics of Wolverine reduce him to a hypermasculine stereotype such as the loner cowboy. Yet, the cowboy itself has a long history of queerness, and therefore reading Wolverine as the cowboy does not make him any more legibly straighter. The cowboy drag that Wolverine wears places him well within the butch, queer culture of the 1980s and 1990s. As Chris Packard writes,

> the cowboy is queer; he is odd; he doesn't fit in; he resists community; he eschews lasting ties with women but embraces rock-solid bonds with same-sex partners; he practices same-sex desire. His code permits few 'norms' as defined by his audience of working-class Anglo-American men, but his popularity grants him wide latitude in terms of exercising his queer power.
>
> (2005: 3).[1]

Queer theory helps peel off the veneer of heteronormativity applied to Logan to reveal the queer character underneath, one who embraces non-normativity especially in terms of the representation of his body and how that body is used for queer relations. A guiding principle of this book is articulated by Michael Warner:

> When you begin interacting with people in queer culture [...] you learn that everyone deviates from the norm in some context or other, and that the statistical norm has no moral value. You learn that the people who look most different from you can be, by virtue of the fact, the very people who you have the most to learn. Your lot is cast with them, and you begin to recognize that there are other worlds of interactions that the mass media cannot comprehend, worlds that they can only deform when they project images of ghettos and other deviant scenes. To seek out queer culture, to interact with it and learn from it, it a kind of public activity. It is a way of transforming oneself, and at the same time helping to elaborate a commonly accessible world.
>
> (1999: 70–71)

Warner's rejection of normativity allows for new queer worlds to enter into our experiences. Normativity stifles and rejects while the celebration of non-normativity brings to the surface other possibilities for subjectivities and bodies. For Warner the queer community teaches you transformation. Following Warner, this book considers the ways that Wolverine inspires queer comic culture through his non-normativity even within a group that is already non-normative (mutants). In his cowboy drag, with his porous body, inspiring queer relations, and further stepping off the page to inspire queer fanfiction, the character of Wolverine opens other worlds of interaction.

As Darieck Scott and Ramzi Fawaz write in the introduction to their special issue of *American Literature* on queer comics:

> The ubiquity of the medium—comic books being among the most mass-produced and circulated print media of the twentieth century—alongside its simultaneous stigmatization as the presumed reading material of a small slice of immature youth and social outcasts, models Eve Kosofsky Sedgwick's (1990) now-classic formulation of queerness as both a universalizing and minoritizing discourse; anyone and everyone can be queer, but actual queers are a minority group in the larger culture; similarly, comics end up in the hands of nearly everybody, but comic book readers are a niche (read: queer, nerd, outcast, weirdo) group.
>
> (Darieck and Fawaz 2018: 198).

Darieck and Fawaz employ Eve Sedgwick's work to outline how comics in and of themselves are a queer medium. Despite that queerness, comics do tend toward heteronormative representations of sex and love in superhero comics. As Brian Johnson critiques, exploring the queer subtext of comics

> must now more heavily privilege reader consumption over industry production, even as the legibility of queerness within the pages of superhero

comics requires that readers vibrate between the melodramatic lingua franca of postwar superhero comics and a new more indirect register: allegory.

(2020: 109)

Johnson's critique puts pressure on a reader's acknowledgment of queer subtext in a world of comics that keeps queerness substantively below the surface. By invoking allegory, Johnson argues that a reader would have to be in the know to understand the key to that allegory. While Johnson's article wants to continue to celebrate queers in comics, his historicist reading reminds us that Marvel Comics once declared "there are no gays in Marvel Comics" (qtd in Kvaran 2014: 146). Yet, queerness in comics has a long history even if one was not in the know. Fredric Wertham's *Seduction of the Innocent* (2014) complained about Batman and Robin's homosexuality. Wertham writes, "The Batman type of story may stimulate children to homosexual fantasies, of the nature of which they may be unconscious" (qtd. in Kvaran 2014: 143). While the authors of Batman comics may not have intended there to be a queer reading of their relationship, nonetheless if someone like Wertham could see it, it was probably there for other readers, as well. It is worth investigating the queer allegory of comics.

Within mainstream comics, the X-Men, because of the nature of their mutations and the traumatic attitudes toward them as different, can be read as queer within the larger superhero universe. For example, in the comics trade magazine *Amazing Heroes* #143 and #144 (1988), Andy Mangels writes a two-part history of queer representation in comics. While steeped in terminology of the 1980s, Mangels writes what might be the first cataloging of queer superheroes in major comics, interviewing major writers and artists like Chris Claremont, Marv Wolfman, and Tom DeFalco. Writing of the X-Men books, Mangels notes the similarities between how LGBTQ people and mutants are discussed:

> Here are some random facts about one particular Marvel comic series: approximately one out of every ten people is one of these. Sometimes these people know when they're every young, most know by puberty, but others don't know until later in life. They are frequently shunned by the general populace, and given nasty labels and names by other people. Fundamental Christians call them "against nature" and groups of people routinely "bash" them or kill them. Many feel that they will be the downfall of society, and should be registered and/or put in concentration camps. The characters of this series consist mainly of strong women with romantic attractions between each other, and men who are completely in touch with their feelings. The women have very socially based "masculine traits" while the men have very socially-based "feminine traits." Beginning to see a pattern here?

(Mangels 1988: 45–46)

Mangels makes overt the subtle connection between queer people and mutants. Mangels argues that "when judged by the messages they are portraying ... [the mutants] can and are seen by many as thinly disguised fictionalization of the lives of gay men and women" (1988: 46). While Mangel's goes on to discuss Storm's queer representation, this book explores how Wolverine fits into this queer, mutant world and how his queerness manifests itself through images, relationships, and fandom.

A Brief History of Wolverine in Comics

This book focuses on Wolverine in comics and fandom, so my analysis will focus on Wolverine on the page rather than his other media representations. Wolverine first appeared in *The Incredible Hulk* #180 published in October 1974 as a cameo at the end of the issue. His full appearance occurred in *The Incredible Hulk* #181 published the next month. Wolverine's creation was a group effort. Originally conceptualized by Roy Thomas, Thomas enlisted Len Wein, John Romita, Sr., and Herb Trimpe to flesh out Wolverine's costume and characterization. Thomas wanted a Canadian hero because there had not been a superhero who had hailed from Canada (Avila 2021: 9). In these issues of *The Incredible Hulk,* the Hulk is fighting the Wendigo, a monster that is conjured forth when a human engages in cannibalism on Canadian soil. When Canadian officials get wind of the Hulk's fight, they send in their Weapon X to intervene. This issue also establishes Wolverine's adamantium claws and that he is a mutant. Adamantium, a fictional metal introduced back in *The Avengers* #69 (1966), was created by Roy Thomas, Barry Windsor-Smith, and Syd Shores as the metal that made up Ultron's outer shell. The significant aspect of adamantium was that it was indestructible.

Wolverine's character truly takes off with his inclusion on the new X-Men team. *Giant-Sized X-Men* #1 was published in May 1975 and included a whole new team of mutants with an international flavor. Written by Len Wein with art by Dave Cockrum, the new X-Men, it was thought, would appeal to an international audience. Storm (Kenya), Colossus (Russia), Sunspot (Japan), Banshee (Ireland), Nightcrawler (Germany), Thunderbird (Native American/Apache), and Wolverine (Canadian) with Scott Summers (Cyclops) as a holdover from the original X-Men would constitute the new team. After this initial issue introducing these All-New, All-Different X-Men, Len Wein would step away from writing duties as he became the new Editor-in-Chief of Marvel Comics, and *The Uncanny X-Men* would begin again at issue #94 (1978), Marvel having not published any new X-Men stories since issue #66 (issues #67–93 were reprints of previous *X-Men* stories). The new writer of *The Uncanny X-Men* was Chris Claremont, who would write the title for another 16 years.

Claremont's development of Wolverine included the idea that his adamantium claws hurt him. Claremont indicated that "they hurt him every time.

Which is why to me, the claws always had to be a last resort. Because he felt the pain every time" (qtd in Avila 2020: 18). Throughout Claremont's run, new details of Wolverine's past are introduced, such as his name being Logan or that he is older than the other X-Men, both of which not only added illumination to the character but also raised more questions, such as: just how old is Wolverine? And how did he get those claws? And, is his name truly Logan? These questions linger for years adding more and more mystery to the man known as Wolverine.

In September 1982, the first spin-off of the X-Men comic franchise was the four-part series *Wolverine* written by Chris Claremont with art by Frank Miller. As Douglas Wolk writes, the miniseries was "a stark, gorgeous, violent thing that indulged *Daredevil* artist Frank Miller's enthusiasm for drawing Japanese landscapes (and ninja attacks)" (2021: 159). The popularity of this Wolverine miniseries launched more mutant series including *Kitty Pryde and Wolverine* which Claremont, with art by Al Milgrom, created in 1984. I will return to that miniseries in Chapter 2. Having a series devoted to Wolverine proved very popular. After the Claremont and Miller series in which Wolverine returns to Japan and readers learn of his time spent there and his love for Mariko Yashida, Wolverine received his own recurring series in 1988. Originally written by Chris Claremont with art by John Buscema, in *Wolverine* Logan does not appear in costume. Claremont and Buscema write and draw Wolverine as Patch, a combination of Dr. Jones from *Raiders of the Lost Ark* and Rick from *Casablanca*. During this time, the world thinks the X-Men are dead, but in reality they have taken refuge in Australia. In his own series, Patch wears a patch over one eye and, amusingly, no one recognizes him as Wolverine. After ten issues, Claremont and Buscema gave the reins of the solo series over to Peter David and Bill Siekenwicz. The solo series *Wolverine* has run nearly continuously until the present day with many different writers and artists (most notably Larry Hama and Adam Kubert).

While Wolverine's adamantium skeleton was introduced in an early issue of *Uncanny X-Men,* it is not until 1991 that it is revealed how he got it. In *Marvel Comics Presents* #72–84, Barry Windsor-Smith writes and draws the traumatic backstory of Weapon X. As I explore further in Chapter 1, this story is pivotal in exploring Wolverine's character and the ways that he is used by governmental figures to fashion him into a weapon. The triumph of Wolverine's character is his resistance to this reductive take on his body. The *Marvel Comics Presents* story reveals how the tension within Wolverine developed; his traumatic past forced him to become a weapon. Logan now has to understand how to fashion himself into the hero he wants to be outside the demands of the military-industrial complex.

The adamantium is a further plot point in the 1993 "Fatal Attractions" storyline. In X-Men #25 (1993), Magneto rips the adamantium from Wolverine's body leaving him vulnerable. While his healing factor eventually heals him, Wolverine is left without the adamantium to balance out his feral side. It is revealed that the adamantium forced his healing factor to always be working and kept his "animalistic" side at bay. As Avila writes, "removing the adamantium, with his healing factor almost burned out, gave [Larry] Hama the chance to dive into Logan's character at a vulnerable juncture" (2021: 88). Many writers comment about how much they enjoy exploring Wolverine's vulnerability. While the popular version of Wolverine is his violence, it's his vulnerability, his pain, where writers find the richest character development.

Wolverine's adamantium is eventually returned to him. However, part of the revelation that occurs in having it removed is that Wolverine does not merely have adamantium claws; rather, that adamantium is actually covering bone claws, something he has had since his youth. In 2001, Paul Jenkins (writer) and Joe Quesada (artist) create *Wolverine: Origin,* which explored Logan's childhood in Canada and revealed the first time that his bone claws emerged. The story was controversial, but further cemented Wolverine's mysteriousness. Although he was born in Canada in the 19th century, his healing factor slows down his aging process. Not only does his healing factor heal him physically, but this is the story where readers learn that his healing factor also heals his mental trauma. The healing factor covers up traumatic memories so he no longer remembers things like the death of his father. In this way, we learn that Wolverine is even more complicated than first realized—his body is working to heal him, whether he wants it to or not. Much of Wolverine's story is an attempt to find his past, a past that his own body is keeping from him.

In 2014, Charles Soule (writer) and Steve McNiven (artist) write the miniseries *The Death of Wolverine.* I discuss this epic miniseries more fully in Chapter 1, but it is worth noting that this story was a kind of end point for stories about Wolverine where his power-set kept increasing. In *The Death of Wolverine*, Soule was able to explore Wolverine over his (in-comic) 130-year existence (at that point). Soule reveals a Wolverine who has lived multiple lives, but most importantly forged important relationships among mutants, friends, and lovers. At this point in his history, Wolverine even has three children—Akihiro (Daken), by his wife Itsu who is murdered, an adopted daughter, Amiko Kobayashi, and Laura, whose mother, Sarah Kinney, used Wolverine's DNA (without his knowledge). Wolverine is still learning how to be a father. While Soule and McNiven write an ending to the Wolverine, good superheroes never stay dead. Wolverine has returned and plays a significant role in the reboot of the X-Men, *House of X/Powers of X* (2019) written by Jonathan Hickman with art by Lenil Yu, as well as, in his own ongoing solo series written by Benjamin Percy with art by Adam Kubert. Wolverine continues to evolve and learn about his past, while writers and artists explore his vulnerability and his nurturing capabilities.

While this publication history traces some significant moments in Wolverine's book history, *Queering Wolverine in Comics and Fanfiction* also serves as queer archive, one in which I have collected queer moments in Wolverine comics that have significant queer resonance for me. My discussion of Wolverine in *Weapon X, The Death of Wolverine, Kitty Pryde and Wolverine, Wolverine and Havok: Meltdown, Wolverine and the X-Men, Wolverine,* as well as various works of fanfiction work as affective queer archive, one in which Wolverine's queer moments have risen to the surface for me as a reader, collector, and fan of comics and, particularly, of Wolverine. As Ann Cvetkovich writes,

> in the absence of institutionalized documentation or in opposition to official histories, memory becomes a valuable historical resource and ephemeral and personal collections of objects stand alongside documents of the dominant culture in order to offer alternate modes of knowledge.
>
> (2003: 8)

As there is no official Wolverine archive, I offer up the beginnings of a queer Wolverine archive full of objects and memory that have presented themselves as illuminating Wolverine's character.

Queering the Fastball Special

Comics are a visual medium that celebrate superhero bodies. Those bodies are usually solid and muscular, a symbol of superheroics in spandex. While Wolverine wears his spandex, it's often ripped from his body because of his head-first attacks. These attacks, known as the Fastball Special, involve throwing Wolverine, laden with his adamantium skeleton weighing upwards of 300 lbs in a 5'3' frame, into an enemy. I want to briefly unpack this example of mutant synergy as this involves the strength of the thrower and the passivity of Wolverine (who consents to be thrown). The Fastball Special is a kind of cypher for this book. Wolverine must make his body vulnerable to the mutant throwing him (originally Colossus, but other mutants like Rogue, have thrown him, too). This move allows him to cover distances using his body and creates a force like a cannonball. It is a risky move as not only is Wolverine vulnerable to the thrower, but he is putting himself on the body of the attacker who sees him coming. By virtue of his healing factor, Wolverine can survive the attack, but he is almost always hurt in the process. As Mike Avila comments, "Wolverine is a character who is defined by his pain" (2021: 7). His healing factor, though, allows him to walk away. The Fastball Special becomes a symbol of Wolverine's representation. It's a queer move suggesting both passivity and activity on the other end of the attack. The Fastball Special showcases Wolverine's body as open to rhizomatic relations; not only is he connected to the thrower and whomever he is being thrown to, but this also links him to the earth, the air, the force of his adamantium-laced body. His body is becoming in the act of the Fastball Special. Ultimately, this book is about the ways Wolverine uses his body to make queer relationships. He does this not only through the ways that he is represented but also in the ways that fans connect with Wolverine—through cosplay, fanfiction—creating queer communities by bringing him off the page. Wolverine is always in process.

This book serves as a corrective to superhero criticism and popular reactions like the letter writer I discussed above, that tends to read Wolverine as only a killing machine. Critical analysis of Wolverine often centers on him as a loner/killer. For example, Jeffrey Johnson situates Wolverine in a Reagan-era conservatism, "like Reagan conservatives, Logan believes in individualism and strong action against criminals" (Johnson 2012: 132). For Johnson, Wolverine is a superhero who is a clear "Reagan era ideal of intensified conservatism" (Johnson 2012: 132). Further Johnson writes that "while most established superheroes embraced codes against killing, Wolverine shared no such moral qualms" (Johnson 2012: 132). Johnson's brief take on Wolverine removes Wolverine from his relationships with the X-Men to emphasize his loner status. While Wolverine does like to be alone, it is his found family within the mutant community that provides him with more of a moral compass than Johnson gives the character credit for. As I will discuss in detail in Chapter 2, it is also this loner status that creates a space to express his queerness. This thread of Logan as loner/cowboy/samurai can also be seen in Neil Shyminsky's work where he points out that "Wolverine's appeal is grounded in nostalgia for a morally absolute brand of dangerous masculinity" (Shyminsky 2006: 397). Further Marc DiPaolo situates Wolverine as

> ancillary to the core plot—the conflict between Charles Xavier and Magneto—but he is also the mutant who is most beloved by the general *X-Men* readership. He is popular, perhaps, because he is in the mold of a Clint Eastwood or Charles Bronson action hero, so he appeals to conservative, macho readers who might not find the comic books' otherwise liberal sensibilities palatable if he were not a cast member.
>
> (DiPaolo 2011: 226)

DiPaolo further criticizes the characterization of Wolverine by opining that Wolverine "cannot overshadow the power of the central story, which celebrates the rights of the individual, and the beautiful diversity of humanity in the face of prejudice, oppression, and the horrors of genocide" (DiPaolo 2011: 226). For these writers, Wolverine is a one-dimensional, hypermasculine killer who is merely an add-on to the liberationist themes of the X-Men. Yet, each of these authors is overlooking Logan's fundamental queerness which ultimately fits quite comfortably in the world of the mutants and their struggles with oppression.

In Suzana E. Flores in-depth study of Wolverine's psychology, she writes that "his traumatic past makes it virtually impossible for him to form secure relationship connections in his adulthood" (Flores 2018: 25). While Johnson's work is at odds with the critical literature that examines the progressive elements in the X-Men universe, as I will discuss more below, Flores's account of Wolverine's psychology, although insightful, overlooks a key aspect of his character: his nurturing of young mutants in which, as I will argue, Wolverine models queer kinship and affective bonds through his mentoring. While it is true that Wolverine often takes up the rebellious position in the X-Men, routinely challenging Cyclop's leadership, for example, Wolverine is always surveying from the margins of mutant culture, creating queer kinships that allow mutants that he mentors to grow and choose their identities away from normative constructs within and without the mutant community.

Gerri Mahn's work on Wolverine serves as a bridge between thinking about Wolverine as a hypermasculine loner and the queer hero I am positing here. Mahn focuses on a key moment in Wolverine's history depicted in the *X-Men* story "Fatal Attractions" (1993) in which Magneto removes the adamantium from Wolverine's body. As Mahn argues, Wolverine is not a dual character, like the Hulk, one that can put away the angry male when it is not needed. The Wolverine, according to Mahn, is always a berserker (Mahn 2014: 124). Yet, for Mahn, Wolverine's recuperation from Magneto's attack also affords him the ability to "redefine his own sense of gender identity" (Mahn 2014: 125). While Mahn points to Wolverine's exhibition of hegemonic masculinity, and his opportunity in this storyline to redefine his gender identity, what is overlooked is Wolverine's vulnerability, something that has always been embedded in the character. In other words, while critics have focused on Wolverine's hypermasculinity in terms of his berserker rage and adamantium skeleton, they have overlooked Wolverine as tender, caring, and vulnerable. His wounded body becomes a site of queer relationality.

The debate over just how queer mutants are is an important one as counter-publics identify with the marginalized mutants, utilizing the "mutant metaphor" as a stand-in for resistance to prejudice and bigotry faced by people of color, those with disabilities, and the LGBTQ community. It is important to consider that if the mutant metaphor is a stand-in for the oppressed, what place does a character like Wolverine have within that metaphor? As Jeffrey J. Kripal remarks about the early days of the *X-Men* comic: "the X-Men became both sexy and 'in'; they were dealing with some of the most potent social issues of the day; and mutation had become and effective fantasy code for social and sexual difference" (Kripal 2011: 177). Mutants (and their fans and readers) have always been on the margins (and at the center, in terms of sales) of the Marvel Comics universe. They are represented as feared and oppressed, defamed as "muties" by the public, and often ignored by the larger superhero community (unless they are needed to help with a universe-defining tragedy). Throughout their history, mutants are symbolically used to represent minoritarian struggle.[2] Critics like Ramzi Fawaz (2016), Carolyn Cocca (2017), and Anthony Michael D'Agostino (2018) write about the queerness of mutants. As Carolyn Cocca writes,

> one of the strengths of the X-Men universe is in its queer families: its diverse characters who are not related through a "traditional" and nuclear

patriarchal structure, but rather who choose each other as family based on mutual love and support.

(Cocca 2016: 129)

Other critics, such as Anna F. Peppard (2015), have pointed out the limits to the mutant metaphor. As Peppard writes, for example,

> the X-Men nonetheless adhere to a set of specifically Anglo, Western liberal values, represented and imparted by Xavier, the wealthy white visionary educator who 'rescues' each of the X-Men from 'savage' foreign locales and relocates them to the North Eastern US, where he teaches them to better serve 'the world'.
>
> (Peppard 2015: 324–325)

The neo-liberal vs separatist ideological battle between Professor Charles Xavier, who believed that mutants could peacefully coexist with humanity, and Magneto, who believed humans would always hate and fear mutants and thus believed in mutant separatism, is an example of both the queer potential of the mutant as metaphor, but also the homonormativity embedded therein.[3] It is a thread of tension that runs through the history of the X-Men even when Professor Xavier is not in a leadership position. Mutants routinely set up isolationist communes, everything from a school for mutant children in the suburbs of New York City to the more recent utopic island of Krakoa in the middle of the Pacific Ocean. Professor Xavier's impulse is to forefront the X-Men as a superhero team that then works to serve as an example of how mutants are "just like" other human superhero groups (and humans). His ideological position proves to be a homonormative one, attempting to create a superhero community mirroring the heteronormative Avengers.[4] As Scott Bukatman points out, however,

> mutant bodies are explicitly analogized to Jewish bodies, gay bodies, adolescent bodies, Japanese or Native or African American bodies—they are, first and foremost subjected and subjugated and colonized figures. If they are victims, however, they are also valuable sources of disruption and challenge—transgressive, uncontrollable, and alternative bodies.
>
> (Bukatman 2003: 73)

While the Avengers represent vaguely defined moral codes, the X-Men, tied to their transgressive bodies, also represent the challenge of queer kinship—not how do mutants get along with the normative majority, but rather, how do mutants get along within the complex and varied community that make up mutant-kind itself? Rather than merely argue that mutants are queer, I want to focus, instead, on how one of the more popular mutants, Wolverine, who some critics dismiss as one-dimensional and over-used, is actually a character that enacts queer kinship and who practices a form of mutant relations in which affection and love become the hallmark of a viable community. As Joseph J. Darowski writes,

> even on the team of societal outsiders, Logan is an outsider. His adoption of the cowboy persona has little to do with his heritage, but may be one reason for his popularity. The cowboy is one of the most significant and enduring figures in American popular culture, and Wolverine is a superhero version of this classic figure. An outsider hero, he does the job others don't want to do to protect society, even though he never truly fits into that society.
>
> (Darowski 2014: 73)

Not only is this book informed by queer theory that examines the queer as a site of utopic futurity through creations of new modes of relationality, but it is also informed by events in Wolverine's story that have queered him while bringing out rabid critique from white, male (and, assumedly, heteronormative) fans.

Wolverine and Queer Coding

Wolverine's queer coding does have a brief history, but this book argues there are more ways to read Wolverine as queer that have been afforded to this point. Famously, artist Esad Ribic's cover of Wolverine #6 (2003) shows an erotically charged stare-down between Nightcrawler and Wolverine (Cronin 2017). On the cover, Nightcrawler is clearly naked while Wolverine smolderingly stares at his naked form. As well, Rick Remender's run on *Uncanny X-Force* (2010–2012) contained more queer relational undertones in the friendship between Nightcrawler and Wolverine. Published nearly concurrently, in an alternate-version of the X-Men, *Extreme X-Men* (Vol. 2 #3: 2013) written by Greg Pak, it is revealed that the Wolverine of Earth-12025 is gay. He is in a relationship with the superhero, Hercules, who is himself bisexual. They are both sent to Tartarus because relationships with mortals are forbidden by Zeus. While there, their relationship becomes even deeper (I discuss this story further below). Furthermore, in the recent iteration of *X-Men* written by Jonathan Hickman (2019), Cyclops, Jean Grey, and Wolverine, along with the other members of Scott Summer's extended family, establish housing on the Blue Area of the moon. It is revealed that Jean Grey's room has openings to both Scott's and Logan's rooms. Wolverine is the only non-Summers member of this Moon Household. As Hickman's story has progressed, Wolverine's representation has opened the character to a polyamorous relationship with Jean and Cyclops. In issue #7 (2020), for example, Scott Summers joins Logan for some late-night coffee and invites Logan on a vacation to Chandilore. Wolverine comments that he will get to see "Jeannie in a bikini." Scott replies flirtatiously, "Scott in a speedo." Wolverine chuckles: "Well, who could say no to that" (Hickman and Yu 2020). The queer, sexual dynamics of their relationship have blossomed in this era of mutant utopia. As Brenton Stewart writes on *Comic Book Resource*s:

> The *X-Men* are pushing more boundaries than ever before. As the mutant nation of Krakoa stakes its claim on Earth, developing a new culture with its own language and asserting its right to independence on the world stage, some mutants are also fighting a more personal battle for unconventional relationships. While the relationship between Scott, Jean, and Logan already seemed to break away from the norms of monogamy, *X-Men* #7 may indicate it breaks away from heteronormativity as well. ... X-Men were notable for their strides in LGBTQ representation with the character Northstar but making two of the biggest characters in the franchise sexually fluid would be an unprecedented win for superhero comics as a genre.
>
> (Stewart 2020)

This is a fascinating development in Wolverine's character, and yet, it has also resulted in homophobic rants from fans (Zaragoza 2020). Hickman's representation of polyamory and bisexuality forefronts the queer potential of mutants in terms of sexuality. While queerness has become more celebrated and overt in recent mutant comics, I want to consider other queer ways mutants relate aside from the important topic of sexuality.

While this book explores the ways in which Wolverine is queered in a broader sense, such as the rejection of normativity that leads to a productive queerness, in alternate universes, Wolverine's identity is more firmly queer. For example, in Greg Pak, Stephen Segovia, and Raul Valdes's *X-treme X-Men* #10, it is revealed that the Wolverine of the universe designated as Earth-12025 is in a relationship with a bisexual Hercules. I want to take a look at that series in brief detail for its use of Wolverine as gay as it speaks to the flexibility of the character while still being recognized as a Wolverine.

When asked about their relationship, Hercules replies, "it is a good story. Adventure! Heroism! Romance!" (Pak and Segovia 2013: #10). In that world, Hercules and Wolverine are the greatest heroes. As Hercules explains, "and the way we slew the worst monster whoever to threaten the Dominion of Canada...we revealed our love" (Pak and Segovia 2013: #10). The revelation of their relationship does not sit well with the gods, even though the gods are polyamorous themselves. Zeus forbids immortal/mortal relationships. Zeus then exiles Hercules and Wolverine to Tartarus where they spend the next three years battling demons. This story is explored in the context of explaining the tragic back stories of the thrown together team tasked with killing evil Charles Xavier across the multiverse. Greg Pak is defiant in his representation of Wolverine in a relationship with Hercules. In one letter box introducing the character of Hercules, Pak writes, "Hercules, Son of Zeus, Boyfriend of

Howlett (that's right, get used to it)" (Pak and Segovia, 2013, #9). Pak's rhetorical move, challenging the audience to "get used to it," indicates the perceived radicalness of having Wolverine in a same-sex relationship—even in 2013. Hercules does not come with the same kind of baggage—this commentary is not aimed at fans of Hercules who is known for his capacious appetites. Rather, this is aimed at Wolverine fans who would balk at such representation.

In Pak and Segovia's issue of *X-treme X-Men* #10, Segovia draws Wolverine and Hercules in a loving embrace, kissing, while the beast they have defeated is at their feet. The frame containing the kiss takes up nearly half the page. Their pose is something you might see on the cover of a romance novel. To hammer home their intimacy, Pak drops other nods to queer culture. In issue #9, for example, Dazzler asks Hercules and Wolverine to infiltrate an evil Wizard Xavier's stronghold by dressing like Xavier's soldiers. Hercules comments to Howlett that "I've always said you should wear more leather" (Pak and Segovia 2013: #9). Pak is subtly hinting at how butch and queer Wolverine has always been whether he's in leather or cowboy wear. James Howlett's relationship with Hercules suggests that Wolverine is not necessarily confined to the hypermasculine heterosexual that some authors are content to write and draw him as. Instead, Wolverine can be and is queerer than he is traditionally written. The James Howlett of the *X-treme X-Men* is just a start.

In Chapter 1, I consider the representation of Wolverine's body in two key storylines, *Weapon X* by Barry Windsor-Smith and *The Death of Wolverine* written by Charles Soule and drawn by Steve McNiven. Each of these stories emphasizes Wolverine's body in terms of an ugly, and what I will argue, queer aesthetic. Contrary to the usual male superhero body, Wolverine's body is considered ugly; he even comments on his own ugliness. However, ugliness is a queer aesthetic, one that broadens the concept of both superhero masculinity and the male superhero body. Despite his ugliness, these stories put Wolverine's naked body front and center. His body calls for a queer reading in which his vulnerability and the opening of his body through the adamantium-bonding process as well as the use of his claws speaks to a cyborg-pig masculinity, one which dismantles easy binaries as to what makes a body and what the male superhero body is for. The cyborg-pig Wolverine embodies a queer, ugly aesthetic that asks the reader to reconsider the ways Wolverine must balance creation and destruction befitting his mutant power of healing and his use of his adamantium claws.

From considerations of Wolverine's body, Chapter 2 turns to Wolverine's relationships with his fellow mutants. His body is central to these relationships for it is in his vulnerability that he models a queer relationality with Kitty Pryde, Kid Omega, and Elsie Dee. This chapter examines three storylines that unpack Wolverine's mentoring and queer kinship. In the miniseries, *Kitty Pryde and Wolverine,* Wolverine mentors Kitty Pryde and encourages her to manifest a mutant identity outside of the X-Men team. In this story, Kitty becomes Shadowcat, taking on a new name and a new sense of herself through

Wolverine's ability to share kinship and love with her. In *Wolverine and the X-Men,* Wolverine mentors the troubled teen, Quentin Quire, who is resistant to his mentoring strategies. In this comic, however, writers and artists depict a softer Wolverine, one who must take on the responsibilities of the new Jean Grey School for Gifted Youngsters. Wolverine is represented as softer, more caring, even in face of a disgruntled male teenager. Finally, in Larry Hama's *Wolverine,* Logan must rescue a robot named Elsie Dee, an android in the form of a little girl, who is a ticking time bomb sent to destroy him. Rather than destroy her, Wolverine opens his vulnerable body to her in order to expand the bonds of queer kinship beyond mutant/mutant relations to a more capacious care for the non-human.

In Chapter 3, I turn to fanfiction to examine ways fanfiction authors queer Wolverine. Often utilizing storylines from the comics, fanfiction authors take Wolverine's hypermasculinity and explore gender and sexual representations not seen in the mainstream comics. By countering "queer-baiting" as we have seen in Hickman's tease of Wolverine's bisexual relationship with Scott Summers and Jean Grey, fanfiction authors are able to explore Logan's sexuality, especially in his relationship with Nightcrawler, Kurt Wagner. I focus on stories from the fanfiction website *Archive of Our Own* in order to trace how fanfiction authors queer Logan and Nightcrawler's sexual relationship. By employing BDSM scenarios, Wolverine is depicted as submissive, consensually submitting to Nightcrawler's dominance. Other authors explore how deeply in love Wolverine is with Nightcrawler, taking the representation of their friendship in *Uncanny X-Men* to a queer space in which they can explore the parameters of love and sex. By taking Wolverine into new queer places, fanfiction authors reveal not only the queerness embedded in the character, but these fanfiction authors model queer possibilities for Wolverine that mainstream writers only hint.

In the Conclusion, I return to Wolverine's place in queer time, a theme that appears throughout this queer archive. Through starts, stops, and retcons, Wolverine wrestles with not only his queer masculinity, but how his body and mind have been sprinkled across time. This is most evident in his role as a father. While Wolverine is good at utilizing his body as a source for queer relationships, he struggles with his own genealogy precisely because of its very queer nature. Wolverine is a queer character who must live with trauma and healing and serves as a symbol of the queer potential of the comic book.

Notes

1 For a retrospective of the queer cowboy in the American West, see *Blake Little: Photographs from the Gay Rodeo.* Ed. Johanna M. Blume (Indianapolis, IN: Eitlejorg Museum of American Indians and Western Art, 2016).

2 For example, in a storyline during the nineties, mutants succumbed to the Legacy Virus, a metaphor for HIV/AIDS. See Christian Norman, "Mutating Metaphors: Addressing the Limits of Biological Narratives of Sexuality," in *The Ages of the*

X-Men: Essays on the Children of the Atom in Changing Times. Ed. Joseph J. Darowski (Jefferson, NC; McFarland, 2014). 165–177.
3 For a discussion of Professor X's early integrationist stance, see Martin Lund, "'Beware the Fanatic!': Jewishness, Whiteness, and Civil Rights in *X-men* (1963–1970)," in *Unstable Masks: Whiteness and American Superhero Comics*. Eds. Sean Guynes and Martin Lund (Columbus: The Ohio State University Press, 2020). 142–157.
4 Examples of this kind of mutant relationality include the uneasy tensions with the Morlocks, mutants who cannot pass as human and live underground. See, for example, Chris Claremont and Paul Smith, *Uncanny X-Men* #169–170 (1983).

1 Wolverine and the Open Body

Introduction: Wolverine and Ugly Aesthetics

The male superhero body is an idealized body. His facial features are chiseled and handsome. His muscles are voluminous. His spandex hugs in all the right places. As Elizabeth McFarlane, Sarah Richardson, and Wendy Haslem write, "the apparent limitations of the body—its mortality, its physical boundaries, its singularity, and its vulnerability and penetrability—are superseded by the excess and possibility of the superhero's body" (2019: 2). Contrary to an idealized body aesthetic, a reader of mutant comics is told again and again that the way Wolverine's body is excessive is within the realm of its ugliness. His body is covered in hair. His features are craggy and rough. His hair is untamed. His musculature and adamantium skeleton often reduce him to standing hunched over. He smokes "stinky" cigars. He drinks too much. An example of this ugly aesthetic can be found in *Havok and Wolverine: Meltdown* (1988) where Kent Williams, responsible for the Wolverine art in the four-issue miniseries, draws Wolverine with over-exaggerated limbs, a perpetually red nose, whiskers that trail beyond his jawline, and two tassels of hair flowing behind his head like a jester's cap.[1] Wolverine challenges the typical ideal of the superhero body in the very unattractiveness of his form. His ugliness contains a capacity for queer possibility. Ugliness, as Yetta Howard writes, is "in opposition to contexts of the ideal" (2018: 4).[2] Howard further connects ugliness to queerness "as a generative category for reimagining gender, sexual, and ethnic differences" (Howard 2018: 2). This chapter takes up Howard's rubric of a queer ugliness as a way to reimagine difference by exploring Wolverine's ugliness as a queer response to the idealized male body found in comics. Far more than other superheroes of his popularity, not only is Wolverine ugly, but Wolverine is depicted naked from behind, from the side, and in the shadows repeatedly.[3] Because of the nature of the way he attacks his enemies, often head on, his costume is left in tatters. In a world of attractive, overly sexualized superhero bodies, the display of the so-called "ugly" body of Wolverine allows writers and artists to represent a different kind of superhero masculinity. In Michael Kobre's terms, Wolverine is "an emblem

DOI: 10.4324/9781003222644-2

of transformation" (2019: 150). In Wolverine's case, his "ugly" body becomes an open body, a site of power through vulnerability, a body that allows him to transcend the human-animal binary in order to represent the capaciousness of bodily possibilities.

This chapter, then, explores the aesthetics of Wolverine's body in terms of its "ugly" queerness in the superhero world. Richard Harrison asks,

> what if it's the case that the male superhero body isn't an ideal that drives some young men to despise their own because they cannot live up to it, but is instead something both impossible and satisfying at the same time, which provides young men within the context of the fictional world in which they're found, a body that is powerful, beautiful, and loved?
>
> (2020: 350–351)

Harrison challenges us to rethink the relationship between the self/reader and the superhero body not as one where the male reader may feel small in the face of the superhero's engorged body, but rather, as a love of different *kinds* of bodies. While it is true that artists render him as overly muscular in super-hero terms, artists also revel in his grotesqueness: hunched, hirsute, gnome-like. The insistence that Logan is ugly and unattractive, feral and grotesque, challenges an easy admiration for his mutant body and asks us to reconsider the male superhero body as a site for different forms of queer masculinity.

This chapter begins with a close-reading of Barry Windsor-Smith's *Weapon X* story, originally published in Issue #72 to #94 of *Marvel Comics Presents* (1991). This story is remarkable for its exploration of Logan's "ugly" body as it continuously displays and dissects Logan's body while it under-goes the adamantium-bonding process. Windsor-Smith critiques the ways that the government normalizes weaponization of the (male) body by making the reader a witness. By challenging the reader's ethical and normalizing stance, Windsor-Smith urges the reader to rethink the aesthetics of the superhero. Logan's queer body resists the normalizing techniques of the Weapon X pro-gram, and the reader is invited to rethink the aesthetics of the body and the power found therein. Rather than a closed body, impervious and muscled, Windsor-Smith presents us with Logan as a non-normative, open body, full of what I call "too-much-ness," an overflow of possibility that ends up resisting the Weapon X program's attempts to mold him. The male superhero body is a fantasy of completeness—nothing can get through the wall that is the male superhero. Yet, in the stories I explore in this chapter, Wolverine's body is continually rendered as porous and vulnerable; it becomes a focal point for the forging of a new kind of male superhero body.

The second part of this chapter picks up with the end of Wolverine. The same adamantium process imagined in Windsor-Smith's work is a problem in *The Death of Wolverine* written by Charles Soule with art by Steve Mc-Niven (2014). Soule and McNiven also focus on the bleeding and torn hero, but rather than Windsor-Smith's vital Logan, their Logan is dying. The adamantium is part of the reason for his death. In Windsor-Smith's, Soule's, and McNiven's work, encompassing the creation and death of a queer, cyborg Wolverine, we see this body as vulnerable and open, exceeding its boundaries. This bodily analysis begins to indicate the ways Wolverine is queered even within the larger already queer, mutant universe.

The Erotics of *Weapon X*

Like Wolverine's adamantium-laced skeleton, Windsor-Smith's *Weapon X* story presents the reader with an origin narrative and a graphic queer representation that reinforces the ways that Logan's body is, at first, institutionalized, but, in the end, resists norms through its queer becoming. Graphically, Windsor-Smith presents us with attention to Wolverine's body. With his finely detailed pen work and use of contrasting colors, Windsor-Smith draws Logan's body, in thinly veiled erotic poses; the viewer takes in each hair, each vein, each curve of musculature.[4] Logan is a 5'3" 300 lb. (after the adamantium process) furball whose most famous mutant synthesis is the Fastball Special, a feat invented by Colossus and Wolverine in *X-Men* #100 (1976) in which Colossus throws Wolverine at an opponent.[5]

The comic story embodies a particularly queer narrative strategy. It revels in queer time. Rather than tell a story beginning to end with a particular *telos*, a comic narrative will go back to the beginning or move forward to the end, sometimes in the same book. A character's origin may be explored 30 years into their publication history, and even that origin story may be revisited later. As Anne Muhall argues, "if queer studies has been organized around a central project of exposing and challenging normativity, the study of how norms are produced, policed and potentially destabilized through narrative has been critical to its methods" (2020: 142). In a "normal" narrative origin story, for example, that of the Amazing Spider-Man in *Amazing Fantasy* #15, the reader learns how Peter Parker received his spider-bite, how those powers manifested in his teenage body, and how the murder of his Uncle Ben by a thief that Spider-Man could have stopped earlier came to motivate his superhero life. All the boxes are ticked neatly, and the reader understands the fundamental motivation of Peter Parker from the beginning. This is not to say that writers have not revisited Peter's story, but that fundamental outline lends itself to a teleologic narrative of the superhero.[6] Barry Windsor-Smith's *Weapon X* story subverts the traditional origin story narrative in significant ways.

Barry Windsor-Smith was the writer, artist, inker, colorer, and letterer (for some of these comics) as Larry Hama points out (2012: 4).[7] In terms of story, Windsor-Smith gives the reader the origins of Wolverine's adamantium skeleton and claws which had never been explained in the character's 17-year history to that point. However, it also unveils a story in which the reader must face a different superhero body. This body is non-normative and open. While comics criticism often critiques and celebrates the superhero body as phallic, puffed up, whole, this superhero body is laced with trauma, blood, and pain. As a letter writer comments in *Marvel Comics Presents* #83, the eleventh chapter of the *Weapon X* story, "I'd say the bio-metallic fusion is totally complete, but that fusion's agony is what causes Logan to become mentally unstable even to this day. Such trauma had to have some permanent effect— even with a healing factor" (*Marvel Comics Presents* #83, 1991). Wolverine's body *is* hypermasculine—muscled and rippling, dependent on the artist—but also born of trauma in its wild, ugly, excessive, hairy way. In a word, he is queer, in the comic world. His body overflows its boundaries: smoke from his cigars, hair barely contained by his mask, claws extruding from his wrists having pierced the skin.

Windsor-Smith writes a queer narrative of Wolverine, one that resists explanation to forefront the body as a narrative. Wolverine, at this point in publication history, is written as a mysterious character; no one is sure of where he came from or how he got his adamantium skeleton or even how old he is. He does not even know himself because of repeated "mind-wipes." He is a man without a knowledge of his past; he is a fractured subject who understands his self only piecemeal, queering the very definition of "identity." In Windsor-Smith's story, the reader never sees Logan referred to as Wolverine (the story is set before he has taken on that moniker). In a vast majority of the *Weapon X* story, Logan is displayed for the reader. He is vulnerable. Thus, the narrative is written on the body; the body becomes the locus of the story. Eszter Szép writes that the drawn body in comics allows the reader to experience the vulnerability that is necessary for community building: "due to their drawn nature, comics can give opportunities to express and to study the vulnerability of the body, to understand differently (with the body), and to respond to the vulnerability of the self and of the other" (2020: 187). Windsor-Smith's story and art in *Weapon X* display Logan's vulnerable body in order to highlight one of the central characteristics of Wolverine: his open body that suggests a hallmark of his character is a fundamental vulnerability that he will use to forge queer kin relations with his fellow mutants.

Logan's agency is buried beneath memory wipes and the remaking of his body into something posthuman. As Rosi Braidotti writes of the posthuman, it is "materialist and vitalist, embodied and embedded" (2013: 51). The mutant body is not one thing. The material DNA (embedded) causes physical manifestations that are unique to the individual (embodied). The mutant body is not only posthuman but is a queer body in terms of its disruption of the "normal" human body, as comics scholars have pointed out.[8] Yet, Windsor-Smith's narrative is not about Wolverine manifesting his mutation (that story is explored even later in publication history with *Origin* [2002] and *Origin II* [2013]). *Weapon X* is a story about how Logan's body is made into something *else* beyond the mutant. This is not a coming-out story, the kind that has been richly celebrated and critiqued by queer theory.[9] Rather, Windsor-Smith provides the reader with a narrative about a specific queer body and how that queerness exists beyond that of binaries.

Barry Windsor-Smith's story circles around the problem of the cyborg body. Donna Haraway writes that "a cyborg is a cybernetic organism, a hybrid of machine and organism, a creature of social reality as well as a creation of fiction. Social reality is lived social relations" (2000: 291). As Mark Oehlert writes, "a perfect example of the simple controller/implant cyborg is [...] Wolverine. [...] his primary cyborg system is surgically attached metal" (2000: 114). As Oehlert explains, the problem of the cyborg hero is twofold:

> Violence, as a cyborg issue, is a double-edged sword. One edge cuts into society's fears and desires concerning the present level of crime. These cyborg heroes are taking on the drug lord and the terrorists who are keeping us up at night worrying for our safety. Not only are they meeting them head on, but with regenerative tissue and psionically-created weapons, they are violently and graphically destroying the criminals.
>
> (2000: 117)

While it may be exciting to read this kind of hyper-violence, the other side of the cyborg problem has to do with the cyborg's integration into humanity:

> Are these images of our postmodern Frankenstein monsters? If these cyborgs are so powerful, then how do we as normal (?) *Homo sapiens* stand a chance if they ever turn on us. In comic books creatures have been created that are beyond the control of anyone. The fictional Weapon X programme is a prime example.
>
> (2000: 118)

As Oehlert outlines, if the human can control the violence of the cyborg, then the cyborg is positively valued. If that control is lost, the cyborg becomes truly othered, no longer an object. Too much agency for a cyborg means ultimately death for humanity.

While Oehlert is concerned with the problem of the cyborg turning on humanity, Donna Haraway argues that the human is *already* cyborg. For Haraway, the cyborg is

> wary of holism, but needy for connection—they seem to have a natural feel for united front politics, but without the vanguard party. The main trouble with cyborgs, of course, is that they are the illegitimate offspring of militarism and patriarchal capitalism, not to mention state socialism. But illegitimate offspring are often exceedingly unfaithful to their origins. Their fathers, after all, are inessential.
>
> (2000: 293)

Like Haraway, the *Weapon X* story sees the cyborg born in its martial glory, yet Logan becomes cognizant of his own political progressivism. Rather than condemn the cyborg as a violent miscreant, Windsor-Smith explores the making of the cyborg and how "it emerges where the boundary between human and animal is transgressed" (Haraway 2000: 293). Already a mutant, Logan also becomes a cyborg during Windsor-Smith's story. His "illegitimacy" is located in his queerness, an agential move that throws off militarism and capitalism. In other words, while at first glance, the Weapon X cyborg is a docile body in a Foucauldian sense, one that is made purely as object for militaristic/patriarchal aims, Logan also overcomes any kind of monolithic programming to embrace his liminality. There is also something ugly about the cyborg. As the cyborg transcends the human body, its depiction of metal parts and glowing robotic eyes reveals its abjectness to a human world invested in a false ideology as to what constitutes the human. Thus, if binary thinking is another kind of normativity, then the "ugly" cyborg-queer pushes past binaries to embrace both/and. When the Logan cyborg overrides its creators' normalization, it becomes the queer cyborg capable of inventing new subjectivities.

Narratively, then, Logan is a queer subject in this story, even when he is not fully in control. He resists authoritative structures to embrace his queerness in order to survive. Windsor-Smith's *Weapon X* story then presents us with a queer participation as the reader is witness to the triumph of the queer body. Power cannot completely disrupt queerness no matter how hard it tries. In the end, the reader celebrates this "ugly" cyborg, queer body, Logan's escape is earmarked by his nudity as he wanders off into the mountains.

Weapon X and the Resistant Body

In case the reader is unfamiliar with the *Weapon X* storyline, the following is a brief synopsis. Before Logan becomes the superhero known as Wolverine and has his adamantium-laced skeleton, he is living as a drifter, having been dismissed from his position with the Canadian government for a violent incident and recurrent psychological problems. His role as drifter is another "ugly" aspect of his story. Drifters have no social use, and therefore, society defines them as useless. Logan is in a liminal space, living in a low-rent motel and pondering his next move. This story takes place before he has become a member of the X-Men, as well. Logan has a premonition that something is about to happen to him. While he is deciding to escape the small town where he is holed up thinking he may head for the Yukon or the Klondike, the story cuts to an unnamed Professor (not Professor Xavier, though an equally bald one) who is gathering fellow scientists to assist him in a new project. He chooses Dr. Abraham Cornelius and Carol Hines—both are unaware of the extent of the experiment, but both need the work. The story then cuts to Logan being attacked, tranquilized, and kidnapped as he is leaving a bar. His kidnappers deliver him to the lab of the Professor. The reader is then met with scenes of

Wolverine immersed in a tank, hooked up to tubes and wires, unconscious. During the procedure of feeding liquid adamantium into his body, his body resists. In the process, the staff along with the Professor realize that Logan is a mutant. Whomever is funding this experiment, an unnamed third-party whom the reader never meets, knows that Logan is a mutant, and we discover that his status as a mutant is why he was wanted for the program in the first place. The rest of the story charts how the medical portion of the procedure eventually succeeds; the scientists then advance to brainwashing him. Logan will no longer have memories of his past life and he will only respond to their command. The mind-wipe is at first successful, but eventually Logan resists. In the end, Logan escapes, having possibly killed those responsible for his radical bodily change. Windsor-Smith leaves it up to the reader as to whether Logan kills them. The final panels depict a naked Logan wandering away into the snow-laden mountains.

While the story's themes revolve around government manipulation of an unwilling mutant and the making of that body into a weapon, Windsor-Smith continually focuses on the transformation of the body itself. While the work of Michel Foucault is well-worn, it is still helpful in thinking about the body in a disciplinary society. In *Discipline and Punish,* Foucault argues that the human body is constantly surveilled through a series of disciplinary actions. These disciplines shape the body into a normative product: the docile body. As Foucault writes, "a body is docile that may be subjected, used, transformed, improved" (1991: 136). This docile body then is studied, shaped, and punished throughout a human's life, all for the purpose of becoming economically useful for those in power.

Upon Logan's capture and deliverance to the Weapon X program, Logan's body is turned into a docile body through punishment, surveillance, and discipline (in the form of experimental science). The reader gazes upon a prone body, poked and prodded. It is a body to be used and shaped. An important aspect of Foucauldian panopticism, the form of surveillance that disciplinary society enacts, is that those under surveillance are constantly being surveilled and thus become the "power situation in which they are themselves the bearers" (Foucault 1991: 201). With Logan kept drugged and memory-wiped, he is never aware of how his body is transformed into a docile body; the Professor and Cornelius strip away "Logan" to become a "beast" that only reacts to the stimuli given to him. For example, Weapon X (the name Logan receives as a docile body) is put into a field while hungry wolves are set upon him. Rather than flee or talk to them to calm them (his ability to talk to animals is an under-discussed element of his character),[10] he merely slices them apart, slaughtering the pack as he has been programmed to do (Windsor-Smith 2012: 49–51).

Graphically, many of the panels focus on Wolverine's naked body. He is submerged in his tank with needles and tubes piercing his skin. At times, the viewer is presented with a picture of the whole body—the reader gets a sense of the full array of the making of Logan into a docile body. In a two-panel sequence, the reader sees the top half of Wolverine's naked body, the tubes snaking from off panel into his torso and head, his arms, and abdomen. Employing an ugly aesthetic to underscore the ways Logan is becoming Weapon X, Windsor-Smith colors the panel in tones of orange, unnatural colors for a body; science lab lights are illuminating the scene. The second panel takes an expanded wide-angle look at the procedure being done. This time Wolverine's body is rendered in skin tones, and the reader can see his entire body framed by the panel. But, in this panel, the tank water is rendered in pinks with the tubes and needles now shown in shades of red. The color change allows the reader to focus on the prone body, submerged, unconscious, acted on. It is a pierced body, penetrated. It is an adult-sized fetus, waiting for new life in its technological womb. The reader's eyes are not only drawn to the body, but because of the use of purples and pinks and the way they contrast with Logan's body, the reader sees the lengths of penetration done by these needles and tubes. Rising from his back like the scales of a Stegosaurus, tubes and needles snake from his spine while bubbles churn all around him. The kineticism of the lights and bubbles in the two panels reveal the lengths the scientists are going to create this new weapon (Windsor-Smith 2012: 17).

The reader is a witness to the torture done to Logan's body. The irony in these images exists in not only the ways these experiments reveal an ever-evolving body, but in how these piercings will forever create a character defined by this procedure. In the eyes of the program, Logan will become an efficient machine in which "the individual body will become an element that may be placed, moved, articulated on others" (Foucault 1991: 164). These experiments make a new body. The ultimate plan for the Weapon X program is to make an army of adamantium-laced soldiers to be deployed without worrying about the individual's resistance.

While the efforts of the Weapon X program are to create the normalized body under constant surveillance, the queer body ultimately cannot be fully contained and resists normalization. The Weapon X program has *made* Weapon X, his resistance emerges as a product of their attempts at normalizing. His body, however, overflows in its excess. Logan's body does not conform to the boundaries of its skin. For example, despite shaving Logan before delivery to the facility housing the Weapon X program, Logan's hair returns. The thugs who kidnap him comment:

"Who shaved the patient?"
"I did"
"Whadja use poultry shears?"
"What?"
"Look at the poor guy…not exactly haute coiffure."
"That's really weird…I shaved him twenty minutes ago, and he was smooth as a cue ball." (15)

His quickly returning hair should be a clue for those in the Weapon X program that Logan is something more. This *Weapon X* storyline presents the reader with two clashing ideologies. In one, the Professor and his employers want to create a living weapon, an assassin they can control to turn on any enemy without the consent of the body. In the other, the reader and the scientists are faced with the becoming of the queer body. It is through the body itself that there is resolution to this ideological clash. Wolverine's hair not only grows back, but his mutant healing factor kicks into overdrive. Before this abduction, Windsor-Smith draws a Logan that is familiar: tame hair, some stubble, body hair, a body that fits his clothes. After the adamantium procedure, Logan is hirsute, hunched, bursting his skin. His hair has become a wild penumbra around his head. His body is covered in fur. His body seems more laden. A close-up panel shows his eyebrows have overgrown, overhanging his brow, almost shading his eyes in their shagginess (Windsor-Smith 2012: 25).

When Logan regains consciousness for the first time following the procedure, Windsor-Smith presents the reader with a full-frontal nude scene; Logan's hand and knees provide a modicum of modesty. The background is a grid of colorful lights from the computers and sensors reminding the reader of the way that this Logan has been created anew through technological manipulation. His prone pose with nodules and wires attached to his skin is reminiscent of medieval early modern paintings of Saint Sebastian, the ancient Christian saint who died around AD 288. Saint Sebastian is considered a queer icon.[11] As Chris Brickell writes, Sebastian has been interpreted as a "gateway to sadomasochistic fantasies" (2019: 187). At this point in the story, like Saint Sebastian, Logan has become a martyr, sacrificed unwillingly to the ideology of the docile body. As Robert Mills writes of medieval depictions of male martyrs, "the crucial difference between martyrs and masochists is that saints adopt transcendence, rather than eroticism, as a way of handling violence" (2005: 175). Logan's body may not be pierced by arrows, but he has been repeatedly pierced, like a cyborg Saint Sebastian, with ports and tubes and needles and liquid adamantium. The remainder of Windsor-Smith's story explores the boundary between sainthood and masochism through Logan's bodily queer response to his transformation. While the parallels between the pose of the two figures is uncanny, instead of passing into sainthood, Logan embraces his open body as an erotic practice.

Fluids

This chapter is examining the different capacities in which Wolverine's body is queer. While the cyborg body is one way to think about Wolverine's body as breaking down the idea that a superhero body is fixed, stable, and complete, João Florêncio's *Bareback Porn, Porous Masculinities, Queer Futures* investigates "pig" masculinities, a gay male subculture in which men push the boundaries of the body through sex acts which also speaks to Logan's open body. Florêncio writes that "pig" masculinities are

> masculinities of the threshold, gay 'pigs' ground their masculinity in their holes. Unwholly, they constitute themselves through a radical openness to the bodily fluids of others, as openness that troubles the private/public, inside/outside, and mind/body distinctions that have sustained European cultures.
>
> (2020: 79)

Like the cyborg, the pig troubles binaries, pushing even further on traditional definitions of the boundaries of the male body. In the pig's case, their openness to fluids through repeated acts of anal sex is intertwined with a reaction to the AIDS crisis which initially shut down bodies in the name of public safety. Within gay male subculture, pigs push the limits of anal sex, taking multiple cum loads or urine in marathon sex acts in which pleasure is located in the extremes of the act, in the fluids that are exchanged (cum, piss), and in the penetration of the body. No longer is eroticism and power entwined with the penis/phallus, rather anality is the site of pleasure disrupting normative masculine identity as derived from the penis.

Thinking with pig masculinity troubles the waters of hegemonic masculinity, especially readings of Wolverine that situate him within binary gender roles. For example, Gerri Mahn's reading of the 1993–1994 *Fatal Attractions* storyline in which Wolverine has his adamantium removed by Magneto during a vicious battle. With the adamantium removed, writers explored how Wolverine became more "bestial" without it.[12] Mahn's reading of the fall-out from *Fatal Attractions* reinforces Wolverine as hypermasculine; with his adamantium removed, he is "permanently diminished" (2014: 123). Mahn writes, "Wolverine did not have the benefit of duality. He was one man, with a single personality, which had to reconcile itself to a weaker physicality" (2014: 124). The problem with Mahn's reading is that he sees Logan as falling into an easy binary category. As I have been emphasizing throughout this chapter, however, Logan has always been a queer subject that transcends binaries through the representation of his open body. As is evident from Windsor-Smith's comic, Wolverine defies the Weapon X program's attempts to mold him—he will not be a weapon in the service of Power. Rather, by embracing a cyborg-pig masculinity, his body is an open locus of queerness which does not neatly fit into binaries. Because of the emphasis on penetration in Logan's creation, his power is one of openness and vulnerability. His queerness, in this case, is intertwined with pain. Logan's perpetually open holes indicate the fluidity of his identity.

In the Weapon X process, Logan is routinely pierced with fluids, his body has become permeable. It is from this penetration that he derives his power, and the very act that defines him—the unsheathing of his claws—is a form of self-penetration; Logan must continually pierce his own skin to enact his agency as the Wolverine. Florêncio could be easily writing about Wolverine when he writes,

> by receiving and accumulating toxic matter in their bodies, gay men enact their *mutant* subjectivities and affirm their bodies as symbiotic entities. They deterritorialise themselves and become 'pigs', hypermasculine living bodies that—crucially—are 'hard 2 kill,' as one of the tattoos on the abdomen of porn model PigBoy Ruben clearly states.
>
> (2020: 92, italics mine)

Wolverine's subjectivity is situated in his body; his mutant healing factor and his adamantium claws are twin powers representing creation and destruction. He has become "hard 2 kill."

To underscore the pain of Logan's new subjectivity, Windsor-Smith again employs an "ugly" palette, this time bright red colors, that draw the eye of the viewer. Upon Wolverine waking up from the adamantium procedure, he stares blankly at his hands. Suddenly, blood begins to gush from the port sites. Windsor-Smith draws our attention to the blood using a bright red, organic color, as Wolverine is set in the foreground with cold-colored machinery behind him. The process cannot contain him—the blood spurts from his wrists as tubes disconnect. Logan is in agony—the panel frame cannot contain him as he first reels back from the pain in his hands, his face is cutoff by the frame. In the next panel, he lurches forward, hiding his face, as his wrists continue to spurt blood (Windsor-Smith 2012: 27). The erotics of the scene cannot be denied, either. The spurts of blood indicate the erotic power of fluids as his agony can also be read as ecstasy.

Windsor-Smith reorients the semiotics of Wolverine's claws. He waits for a page before the blood-covered claws emerge from his skin with a "SHCLUK"; this wet onomatopoeia is a sound indicator of the emerging claws, red with blood, as again Logan is shown to reel away from his upraised claws. The next panel zooms in on two of the claws, a purple background brings the red of the blood into even more relief as they drip from the newly adamantium-laced claws that have become a hallmark of the character. What is usually a "wow" factor for Wolverine, a sign of his imperviousness in a fight, is here represented as full of eroticism and pain. His open body reveals his vulnerability; his strength is found in how much of the pain he can take. When Wolverine unsheathes his claws, the sound is usually rendered as "SNIKT," a sound like multiple switchblades emerging as once. Windsor-Smith writes "SHCLUK," reminiscent of something from horror comics, almost like an object emerging from the mud (Windsor-Smith 2012: 28). It is wet, slow, piercing—not the metallic ding of a "SNIKT." Logan is only learning he has claws here, and his open body has become more real. Each time he uses his claws, he pierces his skin; their emergence is a callback to his new body.

The reader, then, focuses on the blood, beginning to recognize that even though his claws are what makes Wolverine so "cool"—that "SNIKT" sound of his emerging claws bleeding into popular culture—the aspect of Wolverine that readers have grown to demand and love was born by the insertion of tubes and needles, a liquid metal driven into his body. Logan's pig-cyborg body is the "experience of the threshold" in which he becomes ever-evolving (Florêncio 2020: 166). Although the Professor and Cornelius think that they have made a weapon, what they have done is created a new kind of masculinity, one that is grounded in the bodily penetration of adamantium resulting in Logan's open body. Logan's sense of his self, his use of his claws and his healing factor, vacillates between "self-obliteration and creative becoming" (Florêncio 2020: 178). As I examine at the end of this chapter, the adamantium is also poisonous—his healing factor is keeping it from killing him. He is self-obliterating and self-healing continuously while he is alive.

Wolverine and Biopolitics

With Logan's porous body in place, Windsor-Smith explores the queer body's resistance to power. The Professor corrects Cornelius, his main lab assistant, when Cornelius calls Logan a monster. Instead, the Professor insists that they have made a "beast," unlocking what is within Logan all along.

> "No, not a monster exactly," says the Professor.
> "Devil with that; it's a mindless murdering animal," Cornelius cries out.
> "Uhm…Yes. But can we make him behave?" the Professor queries.
> (Windsor-Smith 2012: 31)

The point of the Weapon X experiment is not only to bond adamantium with bone, but also to be able to control the subject of that bonding process. Capitalizing on Wolverine's past behaviors—his drunken fights, his attitude of sacrifice (or martyrdom) in war—the Professor has decided to shape that life into something the government deems useful. Logan will be their beast.

The goal of the Weapon X program is carceral: the body is trapped in the institution that birthed it. Because of mind-wipes and the electronic gear he wears on his head that keeps him focused on his prey, Logan has become "the disciplinary form at its most extreme" (Foucault 1991: 293) in which "the carceral texture of society assures both the real capture of the body and its perpetual observation" (Foucault 1991: 304). Within the overlap of the binary-smashing cyborg and the open body of pig masculinity is the challenge to this normalizing biopolitics that decides what kind of life is worth living. Logan embodies a queer corporeality, a body that "doesn't cohere according to cis-centric, sexually dimorphic, ableist conceptions of somatic normalcy" (Malantino 2019: 165). With his porous body, one that is poisoning him at the same time he is becoming, Logan's body has become cyborg-pig. He is no longer just a mutant; his is a new kind of *bios*. While the Weapon X program has made him into a weapon, the drama of the text asks how he can overcome that programming. As well, *Weapon X* explores what kind of life there is for Logan. In other words, who gets to say what is a (superhero) life? In this case, the Weapon X program has decided to reshape the individual into something that they can control, a pawn on a chessboard. The biopolitics of this is clear: seeing Logan using his life as he sees fit, larger Powers decide to take that from him. Controlling one's death, in their estimation, should be the job of government. By deciding that the way Logan is living his life is useless and "godforsaken: in its pursuits" (Windsor-Smith 2012: 36), they now will shape that purpose. Now, as the Professor opines, they have "the most formidable tactical weapon ever conceived" (Windsor-Smith 2012: 36).

Windsor-Smith presents readers with the dilemma of who uses the superhuman body and for what purpose. Despite his service to the Canadian government, Logan is still too much of a loose cannon. His body, even within the boundaries of service, is too much. He must be made to conform. Logan's body is too queer as it resides within liminal spaces where it cannot be of use to governmental persuasion. He seeks out bars, alleys, and isolation in the wilderness. None of these spaces are productive for a body like his. Instead, the governmental attitude is that his is a body that must be contained, shaped, worked upon. The queer body, then, challenges its containment, and thus, the drama of the story is how Logan's open body can break from attempts of constraint placed upon it. The Professor and his Experiment X program have made Logan's body even more queer and given him the tools to dismantle his attempt at shaping him.

In the process of infusing adamantium into Logan on a molecular level and attempting to erase his being, Professor, Dr. Cornelius, and Miss Hines force his body to manifest its queerness; it's a forced coming out. His queer body should have been evident in the process itself. Repeatedly, the equipment cannot handle what is being done to Logan. When he is kidnapped, for example, the usual dose of tranquilizer does not work, so they must tranquilize him again and beat him unconscious. During the infusion of adamantium, the tanks of liquid adamantium are drained. When Logan awakens, the life-support tubes pop off while blood spurts from his hands. While attempting to brainwash him, the electrical systems begin to spark and overload. Logan repeatedly wakes up during procedures to fight against his keepers. These are all signs of how the M/machine cannot contain him even when he is not consciously fighting back. This institutionalization and victimization of Logan cannot stop his queer, mutant body. Logan's body—now laced with adamantium, which, according to the Professor, has now reverted Logan to his "natural" bestial state—will also utilize the process to become something new, something queerer. This cyborg-pig Logan, now made of metal and flesh, has become even more posthuman than in his original mutant-state.

In the final arc of the story, thinking they have him under mind control, the Professor, Cornelius, and Hines convince Logan that he has escaped in order to see the damage he can cause. In what he thinks is his final battle, Logan breaks into the monitoring station killing Cornelius. During the fight with the Professor, Logan repeatedly shouts, "I am Logan" and "I am a man," despite the Professor's insistence that he is an "animal" (Windsor-Smith 2012: 100). In these scenes, Logan has emerged from a fire caused by spilling fluids and sparking electrical wires. All of his hair has been burned off. He is naked, again, and Windsor-Smith has drawn him truly looking monstrous. His pink flesh retains some tufts of hair, and his skin looks crisped, still smoking. He almost looks glued together with such unnatural skin. His ugly body is barely contained in these panels, either. The monstrosity he is represented as confronts the reader with rethinking the boundaries of his identity as "Logan" and "man." These panels cut him off, showing only half a face or the action of his body, but never his full form. Meanwhile, these same panels draw close on the Professor's face. The action sequences remind the reader of the struggle within him. Even though this is a simulated fight done through his VR-helmet, Logan insists on his name. He may look the monster, and the reader cannot help but see his deformity as ugly and monstrous, but he is embdodies hybridity. This tension will follow Logan through much of his future story in Marvel comics.

The monster then is a creation of Power, but this does not mean that the monster is unable to fight back for its own sense of queerness. The assumption is that the monster is a sounding board for a culture's fears. While this is true for one reading of Logan, the fear here being what happens when the superhero is reduced to a weapon without ethical sense, Windsor-Smith is also reminding the reader that the monster has agential power. It has a voice and a sense of self regardless of the ways culture has placed them in liminal spaces. These action sequences pose powerful questions: what is Logan now after this shaping by institutions outside himself? What will allow him to maintain a semblance of self?

His virtual revenge on his captors has returned Logan to self-awareness. Windsor-Smith returns the reader to Logan's sense of agency through dialogue. As a sign that Logan has returned, his clipped sentences return to the dialogue boxes. However, Logan is also slowly becoming aware of his new body. During the simulation, he thinks he has "knifed" Cornelius until he sees his claws unsheathe. The reader is again placed in a position of knowledge that the protagonist does not have. Throughout this story, the reader has been in a position of witness. The reader now understands the lengths that power will go to weaponize the individual, to make the docile body which will conform with the institution's wishes. While the reader was placed in a position of perspective with his captors, the reader is now back in Logan's head.

In the end, Logan escapes. Windsor-Smith does not show the reader if he actually kills the three scientists once he is freed from the VR simulation, only that he has slashed through their door. Is he now a monster bent on revenge? It is unclear. However, in the final piece of the story, "Interlude and Escape," Windsor-Smith draws Logan walking naked through blowing snow. Overlaid with the images is a conversation between Cornelius and Hines. Hines is the innocent; she wants to know more about Logan and how he got to the facility. She expresses pity and regret for the treatment Logan is receiving once she learns he has not volunteered for Project X. Again, the reader lingers on the body—now healed and hirsute—this time caked with ice and snow. He has returned to the wild, assumedly the Canadian wilderness he had wished to return to at the beginning of the story. The last three panels give us a rear-view of the naked Logan trudging through the snow. His muscles work, his hair is blown forward from the winds behind him. The queer Logan reminds the reader of the centrality of his body as a source of his power and agency. He will now make himself anew, despite these attempts to normalize him. Logan's body will become the locus of queer mutant relations. Windsor-Smith has called the reader to be a witness to this mutant body and ways it is forged in trauma and pain to become a cyborg-pig-mutant. In *Weapon X,* Logan's body resists easy categorization in its too-muchness in order to explore Wolverine's masculinity as based in vulnerability and pain. He must now search for balance.

The Death of Wolverine

While Barry Windsor-Smith's *Weapon X* story explores the beginnings of Wolverine's body, Charles Soule's (writer) and Steve McNiven's (artist) *Death of Wolverine* (2014) explores the end of Logan's queer body. In *The Death of Wolverine,* Logan is not worried about a future, he knows he must face down a certain death. His death allows him to revisit his history through the vulnerability and breakdown of his very body. *The Death of Wolverine* mirrors *Weapon X* in its representation of Logan's open body, though, rather than Windsor-Smith's concern with beginnings, Soule and McNiven focus on endings and how to memorialize Logan's queer body.

Vulnerability is at the forefront of Soule's and McNiven's story in that Wolverine's body is falling apart. As Esther Szép writes, "human bodies in their diversity are seen and experienced as vulnerable in a number of ways, however, vulnerability is always experienced in a dialogue, because it always elicits a response" (2020: 3). While superhero deaths may be *passe* at this point—readers *know* that the hero will return, *The Death of Wolverine* treats Logan as if his death is a certainty. But, even more than that, this miniseries spends time traveling with the dying. I would argue that this is a queer response to the normative life-giving of the traditional male superhero. In other words, the expectations of the male superhero are that he will save the day, he will rescue a future and cement his place in it. In *The Death of Wolverine,* the writing and art situate the reader deeply in death and a protracted death at that. Logan does not die in battle nor is he lost in space; rather, his death is shown in detail, centering on his open body.

Wolverine's death is a product of him losing his healing factor because of a virus introduced into his system originating in the Microverse.[13] Unable to find a cure for his failed healing factor, Wolverine learns that a bounty has been put on his head. Wolverine is to be captured alive and a number of bounty hunters from Logan's past have come to hunt him down.

Soule and McNiven's four-issue *Death of Wolverine* story shows Logan taking proactive steps to find out who is after him, even with the knowledge that he is facing death. After learning from the Fantastic Four's resident scientist, Reed Richards, that Wolverine is facing "heavy metal leukemia," Reed furthers warns him, "If you don't get endocarditis from all the bacteria you pull into yourself every time you use your claws" (*Death of Wolverine* #1, 2014). Reed Richard's prescription: do not use the claws. Without his healing factor, and now his inability, to use his claws, Wolverine is faced with a new challenge to his sense of identity, for what is this superhero character without his healing factor or adamantium claws?

Of course, despite the doctor's orders, he will continue to use his claws as he returns to key places in his publication history. He faces down a slew of bounty hunters at his cabin in the wilderness that he shared with Silver Sable (Soule and McNiven, 2014: *Death of Wolverine* #1). He faces down arch-enemies Viper and Sabretooth in Madripoor (Soule and McNiven, 2014: *Death of Wolverine*: #2). Further, he teams up with Kitty Pryde to fight Ogun in Japan (Soule and McNiven, 2014: *Death of Wolverine* #3). Finally, he returns to a Weapon X facility in Paradise Valley, Nevada to face one of the masterminds behind the bounty on his head, Dr. Abraham Cornelius, who the reader has met in *Weapon X* (Soule and McNiven, 2014: *Death of Wolverine* #4). The subplot is that Cornelius has been capturing elite athletes and highly decorated soldiers in an attempt to improve on the adamantium-bonding procedure started by the Professor. Unfortunately, those kidnapped keep dying in the process; Cornelius has decided he needs Logan's blood for its healing factor, something Cornelius does not realize that Wolverine has lost. Upon confronting Cornelius, Wolverine destroys the lab where three captives are undergoing the adamantium-bonding procedure. Wolverine saves them and slashes open the liquid adamantium tanks causing them to spill the liquid adamantium over his body. He emerges in the sunset, in pursuit of Cornelius who is trying to escape via a helicopter on the roof. Cornelius dies having taken a large shard of glass to his intestine during Logan's initial confrontation with him and has bled out. With the adamantium hardening around his body, encasing him in the very thing that is a central part of his heroic identity, the adamantium-cocoon kills Wolverine as he kneels before a brilliant sunset.

As a mirror of the *Weapon X* storyline, this story also focuses on the body. In many ways, *The Death of Wolverine* explores how Wolverine has made a self over time despite the trauma and technology that tried to make him a weapon as seen in *Weapon X*. As Hilary Malantino writes,

> our selves are constituted [...] through a terse and unpredictable interaction of technologies of domination and technologies of the self, forces of oppression, and more of less successful attempts at transformation and

metamorphosis wherein we realize an always present potential to become something other than what technologies of domination attempted to make of us.

(2019: 45)

Each issue of the miniseries explores how Wolverine has become "something other" than what the technology attempted to make of him.

Issue 1 of the *Death of Wolverine* opens with a full splash page in which Wolverine lays against the cabin wall. It is a similar prone position that the reader saw during *Weapon X*. He is vulnerable, spent. The difference is that this Wolverine is aware of what's happening to his body. It's only after this splash page that the reader sees the flashback in which Reed Richard delivers the news about the sorry state of his body. Rather than the entry of tubes and wires, as the reader saw in Windsor-Smith's *Weapon X*, in this opening splash page, Wolverine looks to the sky, his claws extended, his clothes tattered and blood-stained, and his torso marked with open wounds.

While the text blocks in Windsor-Smith's *Weapon X* were used as dialogue between the scientists, Soule uses them for the reader to dramatize Wolverine's interior sense perceptions: "Scent's on the wind, gunsmoke, blood." "Sounds ... nothing." "Pain ... hands." (Soule and McNiven 2014, *Death of Wolverine* #1). As Sara Ahmed writes in *Queer Phenomenology,*

bodies may become orientated in this responsiveness to the world around them, given the capacity to be affected. In turn, given the history of such responses, which accumulate as impressions on the skin, bodies do not dwell in spaces that are exterior but rather shaped by their dwellings and take shape by dwelling.

(2007: 9)

Ahmed's work stresses a queer phenomenology which "orients" queer people in "non-straight" ways. The comic book must relate phenomenological experience to the reader through word and picture; the book is a shared dwelling. As Ester Szép writes, "dwelling is a dynamic, attentive, spontaneous, and unfinished activity [...] connected to the concept of vulnerability" [...] "dwelling is a relationship among people and their surroundings based on recognizing the shared nature of vulnerability" (2020: 112). By placing the reader within Wolverine's body, the reader travels with Logan through his vulnerability and the pain of his death. As Ian Hague writes, "readers do not interact with comics through their eyes alone; their whole bodies are involved in the *performance* of the work" (2014: 7). Not only does the reader experience the visual aspects of the art, but by emphasizing smells, sounds, and touch (pain), the reader becomes acquainted with Logan's particular body and its struggles. The reader becomes, queerly, oriented into his body. Rather than witness his trauma from the outside, the reader becomes part of Wolverine's story. Rather than a complicit actor to the creation of Wolverine's body as in *Weapon X,* in *The Death of Wolverine,* the reader becomes the queer body of Wolverine. The reader is inside Logan's head for a good portion of the story; with him, the reader will face the disruptive queerness of dying.

While the narrative of this four-part story focuses on key moments in Wolverine's history, the comic graphically places Wolverine's body at the center. His is the body in pain; the reader is faced with the ugly debilitation of a superhero in graphic terms and pictures. In each issue, Wolverine loses a piece of himself. He is continually bandaging his wounds. For example, when he fights Sabretooth in Issue #2, Wolverine bloodily loses an eye. To emphasize his debilitation, in Issue #1, Soule and McNiven offer up a three-panel sequence that returns the reader to the claws. Panel one is a close-up of the claws extended, blood dripping out from the holes in the skin, rivulets of blood wind around and down the extended adamantium of each claw. The second panel moves us closer to the claw-site as Wolverine retracts the claws with a "SHKK," as more blood, thicker, emerges from the act of retraction. The third long panel moves to show only Logan's face in obvious pain; he bites his lower lip with a grimace. The text box reads only "Hands" (Soule and McNiven, 2014: *Death of Wolverine* #1).

It is in Issue #4, however, that the reader is faced with the dying body on display. I want to linger a little on the difference between the depiction of Wolverine as dead on the cover of Issue #4 and his actual death within the pages of that issues. This disjuncture is a queer one in that Wolverine's death is not just an ending. His queer death underscores the aesthetics of a life and Issue #4 attempts to capture the capaciousness of death. The cover of issue 4 depicts Lady Death bearing a naked and dead Wolverine. The cover is reminiscent of the cover of *The Death of Captain Marvel* (1982) by Jim Starlin where Lady Death mourns the body of Captain Marvel who has succumbed to cancer.[14] McNiven's cover offers up Logan's nude body once again.[15] It is significant that Wolverine is no longer in costume in any of these issues as he strips away both his history and overt superheroics in order to stop one of the scientists responsible for his adamantium implants. As José Alaniz writes of death in superhero comics, "this ultimate human vulnerability jars irremediably with the definition of the superhero" (2014: 238). The *pieta* image harkens back to Renaissance sculpture in which the Virgin Mary weeps over the prone, dead body of Christ. On this cover, Wolverine, claws extended, eyes closed, smattered with blood, is carried by Death who is holding his thigh high to hide his genitals—it is both an erotic and sad sight. The reader knows that they have reached the end of this Wolverine's life and they must bear witness to the body before them.

The beatific cover does not match his actual death, however. The cover image does not depict a body encased in adamantium, rather an erotic body to behold, passive, and spent. Harkening back to my earlier discussion of Saint Sebastian, this cover image makes Wolverine into ever more of a queer icon. Each muscle group is rendered in detail, the hair is mussed, a little wild. Our eyes return to the muscular quadriceps, the longest muscle on display— necessary to carry his three-hundred pound build due to the metal he carries around with him. The cover eroticizes Logan's death; he may be ugly and short, but in death he is beatific.

As I have traced throughout this chapter, Wolverine's body is porous, having opened itself to fluids, having been penetrated by the adamantium. As cyborg/pig/mutant, Wolverine dismantles easy dualisms between human and mutant, embodying a subculture of mutant life in which his power vacillates between death and creation, pain and becoming. He is not one thing, as Wolverine is always in process. The twist at the end of this story is that his acts of heroism in which he has saved three of Cornelius's victims has also caused his death. Covered in liquid adamantium that is slowly hardening, he approaches an escaping Cornelius who is dying from his intestinal bleeding. Cornelius screams at the approaching adamantium-covered hero: "I tried to change the world. What did you ever do but kill people?" (Soule and McNiven, 2014: *Death of Wolverine* #4). The reader gets the answer to Cornelius's accusation in the next two-page layout divided into three tiers. The top tier of these final pages consists of six panels that highlight the ways Wolverine has never been a stable body. In each panel, Wolverine is depicted in various roles: as Wolverine in costume, as Patch, the hero of Madripoor, as kissing Jean Grey, as a soldier during World War II, as a teacher at the Jean Grey School for Gifted Youngsters, as well as in his engagement photograph with Mariko. Each of these identities also indicates the ways Wolverine has allowed his body to be open: to love (Jean Grey, Mariko), to a community and family (Wolverine in costume as member of the X-Men), to mentorship (teaching in the school), to action (X-men, war).

The middle three panels of this page show Wolverine staggering across the roof of the Pleasant Valley Weapon X facility as the adamantium is slowly hardening. His death is juxtaposed with the life he loved above him. He will slowly be brought to his knees by the heavy metal. From the left side of the page, the viewer is behind Logan, the adamantium is still wet and dripping. The middle panel is a long shot showing his slow lumber to the roof's edge. In the next panel, the reader is in front of Wolverine as he slowly drops to one knee. The final panel on the right is close-up, the adamantium, more solid, shines in the sun, having finally hardened. This panel only focuses on Logan's now-covered face. The facial features have now been obscured beneath the adamantium. The bottom of the page is one continual panel of the brilliant sunset. The day and the life of Wolverine has set. The final page of Issue #4, with only "End" at the bottom, is a full page of the kneeling and adamantium-encased Wolverine. The adamantium drapes solidly leaving him sculpture-like. The sun bounces off of him brilliantly. His claws are out, but his palms are raised in supplication to the sun. Supplication, rest, repose, bodily encasement: this is the death of the Wolverine.

In *The Death of Wolverine,* Soule and McNiven invites the reader to consider how a superhero faces death. If the superhero book has always been about the impervious body, the body that is in service to the future, invincible, muscled, what happens when it is no longer in service to preserving a legacy? In Wolverine's case, death becomes aesthetics; it is a queer force as it declares that the queer superhero body shines brightly in the sun. Logan's life may have ended on the roof in the setting sun, but it's queerness lives on in the monument of his body.

The erotics of the cover of Issue #4, with Logan's naked body offered up to the reader by Lady Death, is covered over with rivulets of adamantium by the end of the interior of the book. McNiven, Jay Leister, and Justin Parson's cover art reminds the reader of the Wolverine that is lost. With its harkening back to the *pieta,* the cover is sculpture-like, too. Death bearing the body and the adamantium-encased Wolverine at the end of the issue are bookends to an ideology of Logan's queer body—Wolverine's body is erotic in its ugliness—yet, in death, and an ugly death at that, Logan is now a shining memorial. It is up to the reader to decide how to mark that memory.

In spite of claims of his ugliness, there is an aesthetic appreciation for Logan's non-conforming body. The adamantium that made him Wolverine does kill him; the fluid is toxic and the same science that made him, also proves his end. His body has afforded him a proliferation of subjectivities allowing him to transcend bodily binaries in order to embrace pig/cyborg/mutant queerness. It is his body that has always been a source of his queerness, a site for relationality that he will use to mentor queer, mutant youth. Wolverine's queer relations are the subject of the next chapter.

Notes

1 See Walter Simonson, Louise Simonson (writers), John J. Muth and Kent Williams (artists), *Havok and Wolverine: Meltdown* nos. 1–4 (New York: Marvel, 1988). For a queer reading of *Havok and Wolverine: Meltdown,* see Murphy Lee, "*Havok/Wolverine: Meltdown;* Queer Subtext and Nuclear Anxiety,*" Medium* May 17, 2018. https://medium.com/@murphyleigh/havok-wolverine-meltdown-queer-subtext-and-nuclear-anxiety-e1bdcd95d70d.

2 For a historical survey of ugliness, see Umberto Eco, *On Ugliness.* Trans. Alastair McEwan (New York: Rizzoli, 2007). See also the collection *The Politics of Ugliness.* Eds. Ela Przybylo and Sara Rodriguez (Cham, Switzerland: Palgrave Macmillan, 2018).

3 Some examples of ugly Wolverine art include Sam Keith (cover) *Marvel Comics Presents* #109 (1992); Howard Chaykin, *Wolverine* #56 (2007); John Romita Jr. and Dan Green, *Uncanny X-Men* #193 (1985); Barry Windsor-Smith, *Uncanny X-Men* #205 (1986); Rick Leonard, *Uncanny X-Men* #237 (1988); John Buscema, *Wolverine* #1 (1988); Klaus Janson, *Wolverine* #26 (1990); Gene Colan, *Wolverine* #9 (1988); Todd McFarlane, Wolverine pin-up in *Wolverine* #6 (1989); Bill Sienkiwicz, Wolverine pin-up in *Wolverine* #2 (1988). A textual example in which Wolverine's ugliness is referred to can be found in Greg Rucka, *Wolverine* #5 (2011).

4 For a discussion of Barry Windsor-Smith's approach to comics arts see Gary Groth, "The Barry Windsor Smith Interview," *Comics Journal* 190 (September 1996). Online at http://www.tcj.com/the-barry-windsor-smith-interview/.

5 See my discussion of the Fastball Special in the Introduction and https://marvel. fandom.com/wiki/Glossary:Fastball_Special for a full description of the Fastball Special.

6 See Stan Lee (writer) and Steve Ditko (artist), "Spider-Man," *Amazing Fantasy*, no. 15 (New York: Marvel, 1962).

7 For this chapter, I am using the trade publication of Barry Windsor-Smith's *Weapon X* story which reprints the material originally printed in *Marvel Comics Presents* #72–#84 (1991). Throughout the chapter, I use in-text parenthetical page numbers for Windsor-Smith's text.

8 See Ramzi Fawaz, *The New Mutants: Superheroes and the Radical Imagination of American Comics* (New York: New York University Press, 2017), especially Chapter 4, pp. 144–163 and Scott Bukatman, "X-Bodies: The Torment of the Mutant Superhero," in *Matters of Gravity: Special Effects and Supermen in the 20th Century* (Durham, NC: Duke University Press, 2003). 48–78. For a discussion of queer theory and posthumanism, see Patricia MacCormack, "Queer Posthumanism: Cyborgs, Animals, Monsters, Perverts," in *The Ashgate Research Companion to Queer Theory*. Eds. Noreen Giffney and Michael O'Rourke (Farnham: Ashgate, 2009). 111–126.

9 See Mary Louis Rasmussen, "The Problem with Coming Out," *Theory into Practice* 43, no. 2 (2004): 144–150; Jasbir K. Puar, *Terrorists Assemblages: Homonationalism in Queer Times* (Durham, NC: Duke University Press, 2007); and Anne Muhall, "Queer Narrative," in *The Cambridge Companion to Queer Studies*. Ed. Siobhan Somerville (Cambridge, Cambridge University Press, 2020) especially pp. 145–147.

10 For a discussion of Wolverine's connection to the animal world and his connection with Storm because of her bond with nature, see Miles Body, *The X-Men Comics of Chris Claremont* (New York: I.B. Tauris, 2018) especially pp. 26–28.

11 For a discussion of the history of Saint Sebastian as a queer icon, see, for example, José Cartagena Calderón, "Saint Sebastian and the Cult of the Flesh: The Making of a Queer Saint in Early Modern Spain," in *Queering Iberia: Iberian Masculinities at the Margins*. Ed. Josep M. Armengol-Carrera. Masculinity Studies: 2 (New York: Peter Lang Publishing Inc., 2012). 7–44. For an overview of contemporary queer art of Saint Sebastian, see Kittredge Cherry, "Saint Sebastian: History's First Gay Icon?" *QSpirit*, January 21, 2021. https://qspirit.net/saint-sebastian-gay-icon/.

12 For example, see Larry Hama (writer) and Val Semeiks (artist) *Wolverine* #101-#102 (New York: Marvel, 1996).

13 See Paul Cornell, *Wolverine* vol. 5, #6 (New York: Marvel Comics, 2013). Cornell will continue to explore Wolverine losing his healing factor in the rest of volume 5 and volume 6 of Wolverine before Soule takes over for the *Death of Wolverine*.

14 For an astute analysis of *The Death of Captain Marvel,* see José Alaniz, *Death, Disability, and the Superhero: The Silver Age and Beyond* (Jackson: University of Mississippi Press, 2014). 198–241.

15 For an analysis of the superhero body in terms of gender conformity, see Anna F. Peppard's "'Is that a monster between your legs or are ya just happy to see me?': Sex, Subjectivity, and the Superbody in the *Marvel Swimsuit Special*," in *The Routledge Companion to Gender and Sexuality in Comic Book Studies*. Ed. Frederick Luis Aldama (New York: New York University Press, 2021). 90–105. Peppard discusses the gender norms within the *Swimsuit Special* discussing how artist Kevin Nowlan's blocky style "diffuse[es] the deviant eroticism of Wolverine and Beast's connotatively feminine 'butt first' poses" (97). While Wolverine falls under a subversive body, the artist diffuses that subversion through his style.

2 Wolverine and Queer Kinships

As explored in the first chapter, Wolverine's ever-in-process body is displayed as an example of the ways he embodies queer subjectivities: open, ugly, vulnerable, and generative. Vulnerability for Wolverine is something he always carries with him; it is not something he ever overcomes. Part of this vulnerability is linked to his cyborg-pig masculinity as it is embodied in his struggles with pain and trauma that leave him open; his body is both destructive and creative. Wolverine's bodily relations orient him toward solitude, an opting out, as I will discuss below. This opting out also allows for space to cultivate queer kinship with other traumatized mutant bodies. This chapter picks up on Wolverine's body as a site for the questioning of hegemonic norms in his forming of queer relations with his mutant mentees. I will focus on three storylines involving Wolverine's building of queer kinship. In 1984, Chris Claremont (writer) and Allen Milgrom (artist) created a six-issue miniseries that explored the relationship and mutant identity of the two mutants. *Kitty Pryde and Wolverine* (1984–1985) tells the story of Katherine Pryde's evolution into the heroine, Shadowcat. She is helped along the way by a very wounded and vulnerable Wolverine. Set in Japan, the story isolates the two characters from the other X-Men in order that they learn to rely on each other as they grow and heal. While at first glance, this story is about a mentor and a mentee, upon a deeper analysis, this miniseries showcases the queerness of mutants through the forging of queer kinship bonds. By the end of this story, Shadowcat and Wolverine have grown considerably, and the seeds of this story grow in future X-Men comics as Shadowcat takes on leadership roles, while Wolverine discovers his capacity for creating kinship with young mutants. The second story arc is the first three issues of *Wolverine and the X-Men* (2011) by Jason Aaron (writer) and Mark Bachalo (artist), which puts Wolverine in charge of the Jean Grey School for Gifted Youngsters. Wolverine has to juggle between being the headmaster, a teacher, and a mentor for the very difficult Kid Omega, Quentin Quire. This story emphasizes queer kinship as Wolverine must juggle various roles that de-emphasize the violent berserker in order to showcase the queer mentor. The final story arc is found in Larry Hama's and Marc Silvestri's *Wolverine* (#38–40, 1991) which extends Wolverine's queer relations into

DOI: 10.4324/9781003222644-3

the realm of a radical ethics, as he bonds with the android child, Elsie Dee, recognizing her as more than a robot and extending love to her even when she is sent to kill him. I bring these three storylines together to highlight the ways various writers have used queer kinship to broaden Wolverine's characterization. While traditionally Wolverine is depicted as a loner, in the hands of many writers, Wolverine proves to be a capacious mentor who guides young mutants (and androids) into understanding, kinship, and love.

Defining Queer Kinship

Queer kinship is defined as the creation of new relationships not based on heteronormative patterns. As Bruce Henderson writes, "family of choice" has "been used to acknowledge the existence and describe the composition and function of families not defined purely by biological links" (2019: 223). Wolverine's queer kinships are models of mutant interrelations away from the traditional acts of heroism exhibited by acts of the X-Men. Wolverine's representation over the years points to a complex queerness: he is the "unhappy queer" in Sarah Ahmed's formulation, forgoing happiness (for example, each time he uses his claws, he is in immense pain as they pierce his skin) in order to imagine a mutant/queer future.[1] Yet, he also encourages young mutants to understand their genealogy in mutant history while forging their own subjectivities. Wolverine resists queer/mutant homonormativity[2] through the creation of queer kinships; the ways that writers and artists have enriched this long-lived character suggest queerer models of relationality in the *X-Men* family of books.

Throughout this chapter, I will be framing Wolverine's mentorship of young mutants in terms of building queer kinship. Mutants are a queer community set apart from the rest of the human population based on traits that emerge when a mutant arrives at puberty. The Marvel Comics mutants are queer in contrast to the predominantly heteronormative makeup of the rest of that comic universe. Thus, mutants share a common kinship rooted in the trauma of mutation, even though those mutations may allow them to pass as human or result in physical manifestations like a gelatinous body that reveals the skeleton within (Glob Herman) or a body full of eyes (Eye-Boy); depending on the physical manifestation of the mutation, the mutant may be able to pass as human or may be seen as a mutant without the ability to hide. In an interview, Chris Claremont comments on why he thinks the X-Men have endured for so long. He points out that

> I think because, at its core, it's a book about outcasts, about people who are so screwed over in their loves that they have no family but the one that they build for themselves. It's a quest for family. It's a quest for a place to belong, a place where you are welcome among people who believe deep down inside that they would never be welcomed anywhere else.

(Claremont 2006: 80)

Mutants share a kinship based not in blood, but in their very unique biology and mutations and the ways that the non-mutant world has expressed its hatred and fear of them. Wolverine, too, is on a quest for a place to belong, but he takes a queer path to acknowledge this.

Wolverine's performativity of queer kinship allows for new models of relationality, pathways for negotiating a mutant community that risks falling into homonormativity. One of the challenges for mutant comics, and Wolverine in particular, is how to represent difference and create relationships without succumbing to the hierarchical and normative and look outward to form intimacies not available to other superhero groups. I want to invoke Mary Ruti's work on the queer subject's opting out in thinking about Wolverine's actions in this miniseries. As Ruti writes, "there is a tension between rights-based political approaches on the one hand and revolutionary approaches on the other" (2017: 15–16). The defiant subject in Ruti's estimation is the "subject who drops out of the system" and "who is able and willing to turn away from the promise of happiness (as conceptualized by the normative order)" (Ruti 2017: 19). For Ruti, then "we need to enter into a queer theoretical world within which what is antinormative almost automatically carries an ethical force" (Ruti 2017: 28). Wolverine does like to isolate himself; he is a queer subject who refuses. One of the main ways that he refuses, however, is through the forging of queer relationships outside the X-Men team network creating a safe space in which he can mentor mutant students to understand their place in the larger mutant family without sacrificing their own unique mutant-ness.

Within the mutant family, there is a tension between queerness as expressed in mutant's varied bodily manifestations and homonormativity. Mutants relate to each other in the form of chosen family. However, family is heavily weighted to mean specific things. As Cristyn Davis and Kerry H. Robinson write, "within a western context, the normative family has been discursively constituted as white, middle class, and heterosexual" (2013: 42). Because they are *chosen* family, the mutants challenge what it means to be kin through queer relationships. Julianne Pidduck offers a path away from the normative family through the capaciousness of queer kinship:

> kinship offers a compelling language for understanding the power and constraints of relationality, but to think kinship queerly is an elusive task. … queer does not designate a fixed entity but a performative force of transformation or making strange (queering).
>
> (2009: 44)

The heteronormative model of family can overwhelm queer models of kinship resulting in homonormativity. As Lisa Duggan writes, homonormativity is "a politics that does not contest dominant heteronormative assumptions and institutions, but upholds and sustains them, while promising the possibility of a demobilized gay constituency and a privatized, depoliticized gay culture anchored in domesticity and consumption" (2002: 179). As the mutants come together, as they become family, whether it is at the School of Gifted Youngsters or their welcome into more utopic mutant communes such as Asteroid M or Krakoa, there is a risk that heteronormative families become replicated in these new, queer spaces resulting in a stilted mutant homonormativity. The risk is most evident when the X-Men try to act like the Avengers, as is seen at the beginning of Joss Whedon's run on *Astonishing X-Men* (2004–2008), rather than a queer family as is more evident in Chris Claremont's run on the *Uncanny X-Men*. The heteronormative family pattern focuses on reproducing strict gender roles, heredity, continuity, and a closed-circuit of inward-looking intimacy. Yet, Wolverine models new forms of intimacy that are outward looking and undermine heteronormative relations through bodily vulnerability, nurture, and encouragement.

A History of Mentorship

Wolverine's position as a mentor stretches back to *Uncanny X-Men* #122 ("Cry for the Children," Claremont and Byrne, 1979). In this story, Logan convinces a young Colossus that he is capable of great strength by sabotaging the Danger Room, trapping himself and Colossus in the room, and making Colossus use his strength to save them both.[3] It is mentorship as trial-by-fire. It could be argued that this kind of mentorship is hyper-masculine in focus while still allowing Colossus to realize his potential. A clearer example of queer mentorship, however, intensifies in the *Kitty Pryde and Wolverine* miniseries written by Chris Claremont with art by Allen Milgrom (1984–1985). In this six-part miniseries, Wolverine's character resists mutant homonormativity while also complicating his character through queer mentoring and affective care. There is no one way to be a mutant and Wolverine guides young members of the X-Men along a path of being that preserves identity while remaining connected to the larger, queer mutant community. As explored in the previous chapter of this book, the queering of Wolverine is not new; however, besides his queerness situated in his embodiment, it also has roots in the queer kinship relations developed in other parts of his publication history.

Wolverine's popularity does not fully develop until the early '80s with Chris Claremont's and Frank Miller's *Wolverine* (1982), which tells the story of Logan and his relationship with Mariko Yashida, and the six-issue *Kitty Pryde and Wolverine* (1984–1985) miniseries. It is of note that these two stories establish more of Wolverine's history as Claremont and Miller's *Wolverine* (extending for only four issues, in effect constituting Volume One of *Wolverine*) focus on Wolverine's problematic immersion in Japanese samurai culture along with the cultivation of his relationship with Mariko of Clan Yashida. Claremont and Miller focus on the loner/samurai trope while introducing the first overtly queer character in mutant books, Yukio, who assists him in the rescue of Mariko.[4] While Claremont and Miller focus on

Wolverine's masculinity as a warrior, the six-part *Kitty Pryde* series is the beginning of Wolverine's creation of queer kinship, and it is an overlooked text in Claremont's run on the *X-Men*.[5] The queer potential, in terms of Wolverine's expression of emotion and care and the ability to empathize and guide young mutants, is a character trait that Wolverine carries with him through the decades. Not only does Wolverine mentor Kitty Pryde, but he mentors a number of other young mutants. As mentioned, Wolverine mentored Colossus early on in *Uncanny X-Men*'s publication history. Wolverine also mentors Jubilee, a Chinese American mutant, who nurses Wolverine back to health after an attack from the Reavers (1990s). Further, Wolverine mentors Armor, the Japanese mutant, Hisako Ichiki, who convinces him to train her after he falls into a depression following the events of *Giant-Sized Astonishing X-Men* #1 (2008) (2000s). Finally, Wolverine mentors Quentin Quire, an omega-level mutant, and the first male mutant to be mentored starting in *Wolverine and the X-Men* (late 2000s to today).

Wolverine and Affective Mentorship

The *Kitty Pryde and Wolverine* miniseries presents queer mentorship between Wolverine and Kitty Pryde through both representation of their affection as well as visual cues that highlight their queerness. It is a mentoring relationship that reifies kinships through their shared mutant identity, allowing Kitty to forge her own path and realize her mutant power, while at the same time setting up a non-hierarchical relationship which deepens the characterization of Wolverine into someone who is loving and caring, acting from a site of bodily vulnerability. Kitty Pryde is a mutant that can reorganize her molecular structure and "phase" through solid objects, as well as touch objects to make them intangible.[6] She is an important member of the X-Men as she often works as the moral center of the group. Her youth belies her strength. In an important story that showcases Kitty's power preceding *Kitty Pryde and Wolverine,* Kitty takes on a rogue member of the murderous, ancient race, the N'garai, who assails her when she is alone in the mansion on Christmas Eve (Claremont and Byrne, "Demon," 1981). She single-handedly defeats it.

A brief summary of the beginning of the six-part story is as follows: Kitty Pryde, having just been rebuffed by Colossus when she expresses her feelings for him, travels to Japan to save her father. Her father is entangled with the Japanese *yakuza* who he has allowed to launder money through the bank that he runs. In the process of trying to save him, Kitty is captured by the *yakuza*'s strong guy, Ogun. Ogun, it turns out, was Wolverine's mentor during Logan's time in Japan. Wolverine comes to Tokyo to investigate Kitty's disappearance. Meanwhile, Ogun proceeds to brainwash Kitty turning her into his protege and his personal weapon and naming her The Daughter of the Demon. When Ogun learns that Wolverine has arrived in Japan, he sends Kitty to kill him. In their ensuing fight, she stabs Wolverine through the heart with a katana.

Rather than a story in which Kitty needs to be saved, Claremont and Milgrom turn this miniseries into a story where Wolverine must form new bonds with Kitty in order for her to recognize who she is and assert her self-identity—a process that we have not seen before between a senior member of the X-Men and a younger mutant. What guides Wolverine in helping Kitty in this miniseries are his own failures as a hero. By using "failure," I am pointing to the ways in which Wolverine is ashamed of his berserker rage often resulting in an injured body.[7] This kind of failure, however, offers Kitty the opportunity to balance being a mutant with discovering her own subjectivity. As the story opens, Kitty is taking stock of her accomplishments: she's an X-Woman; she has successfully defeated monsters; she's helped save the world. However, she feels guilty that she was unable to prevent her parents from divorcing, and she's heart-broken that Colossus has rejected her love (Claremont and Milgrom, "Lies," 1984). Her identity is initially connected to the men in her life, as she travels the next day after Colossus's rejection to Chicago to be with her father.

One of the important narrative movements of this miniseries is dislodging Kitty from patriarchal hierarchies. In effect, Wolverine queers Kitty by offering her signposts for her mutant identity that allow her to make her path and self-identify without answering to a father-figure. There is no one way to be a mutant, and Wolverine attempts to show her just that by resisting any kind of prescriptive framework.[8] He avoids paternalism and patronizing. This is a queer, intergenerational relationship, one where each party gives to the other, resisting hierarchies and power-plays. As Julianne Pidduck points out, there must be an ambivalence toward heteronormative patterns of kinship in order to rethink queer models. Pidduck writes, "the notion of affective ambivalence, along with an associated attention to fragmented, discontinuous, and traumatic experiences of kinship, is germane to a queer rethinking of kinship" (2009: 442). Here, the fracturing of Kitty's normative family relationships along with the removal of Wolverine as a hypermasculine superhero allows for affective queer kinship as they heal and grow together. They may initially bond over mutant identity, but that kind of identity politics is not enough to forge a new way out of being in a heteronormative (superheroic) world.

Mari Ruti's work on queer theory's defiant subjects is helpful in reading the bond that Wolverine and Kitty Pryde develop throughout this comic series. As Wolverine is represented as an antisocial mutant ever since his introduction in *Giant-Sized X-Men*, Kitty Pryde is a strong and talented teenager, seeking her place in the mutant community. In this miniseries, both characters bridge their generational gap in order to form new bonds and new subjectivities. As Mari Ruti writes, "the subject as a subject of freedom—as a subject of ethical capacity—can only arise from the ashes of the symbolic subject" (2017: 49). Wolverine's wounded and pierced heart and body and Kitty Pryde's brainwashed weaponized body represent the "ashes" of their subjectivity. Since Wolverine cannot fight, he must attend to Kitty's transformation through mentoring and affective bonding. He must be an open, vulnerable guide. While Wolverine is healing, Kitty in turn supports him in his struggle to understand his anger. For Kitty, Wolverine becomes a model of the ways in which the mutant cannot always enact superheroics; her mind and body need to heal and grow while extending understanding to Wolverine's healing self. For Wolverine, Kitty becomes a site for understanding the very limitations of the mutant superhero as developed in the X-Men, and the ways in which Kitty's very subjectivity is a product of both being a mutant and being in the world. It is an ongoing process. Wolverine's mentorship suggests that healing comes within that site of vulnerability. Wolverine is mutant mentor and *not* a "superhero" in the traditional sense in this series at all. Ogun has turned Kitty into a weapon, much like the Weapon X program had turned Wolverine into one. Claremont represents a critique of the logical conclusion of the biopolitics of the superhero: in both cases, Wolverine through the Weapon X program and Kitty through Ogun's brainwashing have been reduced to objects in order to defeat "enemies" as defined by the larger ideological apparatus of normative superheroics. Ogun has done this by reducing Kitty to a child and the building her back again. Visually, this is represented by Ogun tearing Kitty's clothing and cutting her hair (Claremont and Milgrom, "Terror," 1984) to a butch cut. He has made her into his own "daughter." She thrills when he calls her that, "He called me 'daughter.' I feel so proud" (Claremont and Milgrom, "Terror," 1984). Ogun reduces to Kitty to his androgynous acolyte through repeated battle. Kitty and Ogun become joined as "one" as shown in a panel that reveals Kitty's face as a faint image transposed over Ogun's own face.

After Kitty has stabbed Wolverine at the end of Issue #3, the narrative shifts to healing Kitty. It is in the fourth issue of this miniseries that Wolverine steps up to mentor Kitty through the healing process. While Wolverine takes a breath to let his body heal, he encourages Kitty to take a hard look at herself to see the ways in which Ogun has brainwashed her mind and weaponized her body. The progression of Kitty Pryde's character is in realizing her body is her own and that she can control it, including her name. Thus, this miniseries explores the queer ways Wolverine and Kitty can develop to be more than the normative superheroes through practices of affective bonding and care. It is queerly heroic to care for one another.

Wolverine is able to short circuit the cycles of violence and the objectification of the superhero body as a weapon through affective healing and queer mentoring. Rather than let Kitty go through the affective healing process alone, Wolverine will mentor her through it. While Ogun has brainwashed her in darkness (her deconstruction takes places in panels that have a black background), Wolverine brings her out to the natural world to heal her body. Kitty's healing is depicted in panels that are colorful and full of life. In each of these panels, Kitty has Wolverine to mentor and guide her through, and her mentee-ship also contributes to Wolverine's ability to heal himself. Wolverine encourages them to heal *together*.

One of the ways in which Wolverine forges queer kinship with Kitty is through helping her heal from the need for a father-figure who will guide her. As Ruti argues, "intersubjectivity—the always unpredictable, and sometimes injurious impact of the other on the self—is one of the principal ways in which the subject's quest for secure ontological foundations is challenged" (2017: 133). Belonging to the X-Men is a version of ontological security connected to the idea of a leader and teammates. However, what does that do to a sense of self? This story is rife with patriarchal figures: Kitty's father, Professor Xavier, and Ogun. With his ties to the Japanese mafia, Kitty's father has revealed that he is not the father she thought he was. In a moment of weakness, Kitty thinks she needs to run back to the school to Professor Xavier for mind reprogramming. Ogun has seized on her powers and twisted them for his own purposes. Kitty is not her own self in relation to any of these men.

It would seem that Wolverine should become the next father-figure in a series of fathers, one who will rescue Kitty from the troubles her father and Ogun have caused. Or, Wolverine will send her back to Xavier to be re-educated into mutant normativity. However, Wolverine does not do any of these, and he does not make himself "safe." Wolverine and Kitty impact each other. Within the touch of the impact, Wolverine reveals that neither the original Father, represented by her own father, nor Xavier, nor Ogun, are foundations for queer/mutant subjectivity. Instead, Wolverine provides paths for Kitty to choose from—she could go home, she could kill for revenge, she could figure herself out. Wolverine offers her an open futurity without placing himself back in the original Father role.

Wolverine reminds her that she is strong and that she is capable by encouraging Kitty to use her strength: "The trick is taking the hand you're dealt an' winning anyway. It's a decision only *you* can make, Katherine. The most important you'll ever face" (Claremont and Milgrom "Rebirth," 1985). If Claremont would have written Wolverine to be yet another male figurehead that Kitty could use as a foundation outside of herself, it would have been a trite series. Instead, Wolverine undoes patriarchal replication in his mentorship in order to provide a queer kinship that resists homonormative patterns. Wolverine provides affective bonds that short circuit hierarchal relationships and provides for Kitty without becoming a new patriarchal authority. After Wolverine has helped her remove Ogun's influence from her mind, Kitty decides she must confront Ogun. Kitty, looking at the image of herself in the subway car window, reflects:

> Would it have been so bad to live a normal life? Ordinary life? Is it too late to try? Go to college. Meet some guy. Have 2.4 kids. Live happily ever after? That's what other women do—lots of 'em—why not me? Except normal people don't sky dance. I can't give that up. Even without my super powers I'll never settle for what society—or my parents—expects of me.
>
> (Claremont and Milgrom, "Courage," 1985)

Kitty contrasts "normative" expectations of womanhood (college, marriage, 2.4 kids), with her own lived-in bodily experiences. As Margaret Galvan points out, Katherine "actively engages in feminist practice and continually subverts patriarchal expectations with her transgressive body" (Galvan 2014: 57). She can use her mutant powers to even lift her through the air. Yet, as Wolverine has guided her, she realizes that she does not even need those superpowers to recognize there is a different kind of life out there that does not conform to societal expectations.

In order for Wolverine to help Kitty through her healing process, he gives her a number of physical challenges to break Ogun's hold. For both, the body needs realigned with the mind. Wolverine needs to heal from his pierced heart, while Kitty needs to regain her sense of self. This is a new challenge for Kitty. In traditional forms of teaching, the teenager is to learn from the adults. The Xavier Institute replicates traditional schooling. Because of the nature of Professor Xavier's institute, teenagers are welcome, but they are there to learn from those who have bought into (his) mutant normativity. Here, Wolverine short circuits that teacher-student relationship, replacing it with a mentorship model that proves efficacious for both mentor and mentee.

Wolverine cultivates Kitty's sense of being by challenging her to understand her whole body as it is connected to the self. Rather than a Danger Room in which mutants learn to battle the outside world, Wolverine encourages Kitty to understand the way she moves in the world. For example, Wolverine and Kitty take a hard, ocean swim. In another scene, Wolverine has Kitty attempt to hold a sword above her head for as long as she can; in another, he challenges her to rearrange a Zen garden. It is in her perfect arrangement of that Zen garden that Wolverine is able to physically illustrate just how much Kitty has been affected by Ogun's control. As an amateur practitioner of an art that takes years to master, her garden should be disorganized. Instead, she creates a perfect Zen example that only someone who has practiced for decades would produce. Ogun is still deep in her mind.

Wolverine's modeling of paths toward self-identity and rejection of Ogun also come in harder forms, too. When Kitty falls in the snow after a hard hike, Wolverine refuses to help her up, remarking that she can use her strength. She does get up on her own. It is of note that none of these techniques are battles in the traditional sense. There is no hand-to-hand combat such as used by Ogun to brainwash Kitty. There is no power-to-Danger Room battle to test mutant ability. Instead, Wolverine emphasizes Kitty's self. Wolverine queers the path toward superheroic identity by not "fighting it out," but rather understanding how her body moves in the world. When Kitty, in a moment of weakness, wants to go back to Charles Xavier to fix her mind, Wolverine suggests that she is running away from her problems. If she lets herself do that, Kitty will forever rely on the Father, such as Professor Xavier, to fix her. Good mentoring, then, resists creating a situation in which the mentee is reliant on the mentor. Instead, the queer mentorship that Wolverine models is a relationship in which the mentor fosters growth in the mentee in order to understand their own bodily subjectivity.

Through mentoring Kitty, Wolverine illustrates the ways in which Kitty's mind and body are connected and how to realign her body. He desires to show Kitty that she is strong despite her mutant abilities, not because of them. In this way, he disrupts a superheroic emphasis on mutant ability which replicates a mutant homonormativity, to show Kitty herself first, and her abilities as extensions of her. Her powers do not constitute her whole self. She does not use her powers to heal, and he does not encourage her to use them. This is a fascinating move by Wolverine as he does not advise Kitty how to be a superhero-mutant, rather he challenges her to be her own subject. This split in Kitty and her subsequent journey to understanding the self is visually represented on the covers of the first two issues of the miniseries. On each one, Kitty is drawn as straddling the gutter between two panels; she is divided. On the covers of the fourth, fifth, and sixth issues, there is no division; she is drawn whole reflecting the contents of the issues and Wolverine's mentorship. By the sixth issue cover, she can straddle the gutter as a whole self: Shadowcat.

More than the body however, there are also moments in which Wolverine encourages Kitty's strengths and belief in herself, encouraging a path forward to discover her own queer/ mutant identity. Upon their initial discussion after Kitty has stabbed Wolverine in the heart, Kitty laments that she has been brainwashed—Wolverine encourages her to cry: "Nothin t'forgive, kiddo. I understand. An' I figure the least you're entitled to a good cry. Now, how 'bout some breakfast?" (Claremont and Milgrom, "Courage," 1985). Wolverine holds space for Kitty instead of telling her to move on; in this moment of tears and shared grief, they forge new, affective bonds. Kitty needs to grieve, and Wolverine acknowledges even bad feelings contain power; they are not to be denied or suppressed. Wolverine recognizes this for Kitty even if he often does not recognize it for himself.

Naming is also key in this miniseries. When Ogun brainwashes Kitty, he calls her The Daughter of the Demon. Her name is relevant only in relation to his patriarchal authority. Wolverine provides emotional support in the variety of ways that he addresses Kitty. As Kitty is a teenager, she is often addressed in the diminutive: "Kitty." However, Wolverine employs a number of affective names, calling her "punkin," "kiddo," "Kit," "Pryde," and "Katherine." While the use of "punkin" and "kiddo" would seem to infantilize her, I would argue that it creates a deeper bond between them, an *eros* that is not sexual but productive. On her part, Kitty calls him the diminutive and playful, "Wolvie," as well as "Logan," and "Wolverine" (the latter, especially when she is frustrated with him). He is attempting to build trust and her own sense of self; rather than deny mentoring affection for her, Wolverine articulates those bonds in order to show her not only his belief in her, but that he can be trusted as a mentor. These names give her strength. Calling her Katherine, too, is another way in which Wolverine respects her power—she is a growing teenager—on the threshold of independence and adulthood. Early in Kitty's history, she was given the code names "Ariel" and "Sprite." Kitty goes through a two-page debate with herself as to what she should be named. Through Wolverine's mentorship, she recognizes her full range of abilities and dubs herself Shadowcat, no longer a child or a "Kitty." It is noteworthy that when Shadowcat takes over the Marauders in Jonathan Hickman's 2019 comic, she rechristens herself as Kate Pryde and claims the role of leader and Red Queen of the Hellfire Trading Company, a seed planted here in 1984.[9]

Wolverine never forces Kitty to be a superhero; she must discover her path within the safe space that is the mentor-mentee relationship. In the final showdown between Shadowcat, Wolverine, and Ogun, the battle is fierce. Ogun reveals that he wants to defeat Wolverine so that Shadowcat will become his new disciple. When Wolverine exhausts Ogun, he gives a sword to Katherine, suggesting that she can, if she wants, seek revenge on her abuser. She does not strike Ogun down, illustrating that Ogun's weaponizing of her is no longer existent. In the end, Wolverine's modeling of queer kinship has returned Shadowcat to herself. However, Ogun rises up to attack her from behind. She phases so that Ogun passes through her and Wolverine stabs Ogun through her phased body before Ogun can kill them. Through Wolverine's mentorship, Shadowcat has control over who has access to her body as well as how she can enact her mutant powers. Both men now pass right through her.

The queer mentoring process is also recursive. Wolverine is angry that he has had to stab Ogun, his former mentor, in order to rebuff his attack on her. Shadowcat mentors Wolverine:

> You were young when you met—and in the years since, you changed, you grew! Ogun stayed the same. There's your edge. It would've been safe to keep your beast in its cage and let Ogun cut you to ribbons—but you let it loose! You made a choice! Knowing the risks. You unleashed your demon—but you kept it under control.
>
> (Claremont and Milgrom, "Honor," 1985)

The mentee has become the mentor as Kitty comforts Wolverine as to how he can use his violence without it overcoming him. As well, hidden beneath the surface of this story has been Wolverine's own relationship with Ogun. Holding Ogun's mask in his hand, Wolverine laments, "I respected him, Kitty—I—loved him—like a son—whatever I am today, a lot of its because of him. How could I be so blind not see what he truly was?" (Claremont and Milgrom, "Honor," 1985). Much like Shadowcat learning the fallibility of her own father, Wolverine, too has lost the ideal father in his defeat of Ogun. The rejection of the father for both of them further deepens their own bond. Even Wolverine recognizes the mutants are his kin forged in love and mutual support, not by the tip of a sword. Through the queer mentoring relationship, Shadowcat now can mentor Wolverine when he needs support. Even though I have been exploring the ways in which Wolverine has shown Shadowcat how to control her body, it is here in the end that we also see how he has learned his own fit into mutant life and how to control his own body through the recursive mentoring process that produces kinship.

Wolverine mentors Shadowcat into a self-identified mutant-queerness. One of the fascinating aspects of Wolverine's mentorship is that the mentor-mentee relationship is not that of a traditional sidekick. Wolverine's mentees age out of his mentorship, but they are always his kin. He is not replicating himself in their sense of identity, rather he is encouraging them to self-identify. A queer/mutant future depends on their ability to shape it through body/self/power-knowledge, self-naming, the ongoing process of mutant becoming through recursive affectivity, and resistance to the homonormative. Wolverine mentors many mutants to be self-possessed queers in their own right, discovering their contributions to mutant society outside of the homonormativity of the X-Men as a superhero group. His mentoring creates a path for them to express their queer/mutant identity.

As we have seen him mentor Katherine Pryde, we see that Wolverine exhibits nurture and non-hierarchical care; the mentor/mentee relationship proves fruitful for both parties, and as Shadowcat's and Wolverine's histories continue, they become close friends full of love and nurture for themselves and for other mutants. At the end of her essay, "How to Bring Your Kids Up Gay," Eve Kosofsky Sedgwick warns that

> the wish for the dignified treatment of already-gay people is necessarily destined to turn into either trivializing apologetics or, much worse, a silkily camouflaged complicity in oppression—in the absence of a strong, explicit, *erotically invested,* affirmation of some people's felt desire or need that there be gay people in the immediate world.
>
> (Sedgwick 1993: 164)

Wolverine resists both apologetics (represented by Professor Xavier's commitment to assimilation of mutants with humans) and oppression (the human community's hatred of mutants; the internalized hatred of difference) in his mentoring of mutants.

Professor Wolverine

For Wolverine, the mutant-being is not merely their power-set, rather mutant-being resides in an array of queer, affective practices that both confirm mutant community while preserving subjectivity. Mutants can be queer together without oppressive norms. Wolverine has developed into a complex and queer character through his sense of responsibility and care for young mutants by affirming that there is, indeed, a polymorphous, queer community of mutants. Wolverine offers us a way forward in thinking about the possibilities and future of the mutant superhero. Rather than an ideological mutant homonor-mativity, there is a place for all kinds of queer identities under the X-Men umbrella.

If *Kitty Pryde and Wolverine* focused on how Wolverine and Kitty Pryde develop a recursive queer mentoring relationship, Jason Aaaron's and Mark Bachalo's *Wolverine and the X-Men* brings to the forefront Wolverine's queer mentoring through his relationship with Quentin Quire and his attempt to lead a new mutant school. In this later series, *Wolverine and the X-Men* (2011), Jason Aaron (writer) and Mark Bachalo (artist) explore Wolverine's mission to care for mutant children. His nurturing aspect is on full display as he restarts the Xavier School for Gifted Youngsters in Westchester, NY, renaming it the Jean Grey School for Gifted Youngsters, a homage to the dead (again) Jean Grey. He also becomes head of the school. This is an intriguing move as Wolverine has traditionally not been in the leadership role at previous iteration of the school. His leadership roles have come in the form of leading X-Force and its covert missions. In *Wolverine and the X-Men*, he becomes headmaster, and thus all the mutant students are under his purview; Wolverine ends up attempting to care for all of the enrolled students. The risk here, of course, is in not repeating Charles Xavier's homonormativity. Wolverine's strengths as a queer mentor come from his vulnerable body and his encouraging of self-identity within the greater mutant community.

It is within his role as headmaster of the school that he expresses care for the troubled mutant, Quentin Quire. Quentin Quire is a young mutant with omega-level telepathic powers. Part of the tension that drives the plot in the opening issues is balancing the mentoring of Quire with the fight for the legitimacy of the school as Logan and his fellow teachers seek permissions from the New York State Department of Education to even open the school. While Wolverine deals with the legal red-tape, Quentin Quire is also acting out and Logan has to figure out how to mentor him. Wolverine must set aside the warrior aspect of his personality, in order to cultivate his role as mentor. Although this story is an example of Logan "opting in" to the mutant community, he must still cultivate the queerness of mutants within the school emphasizing their uniqueness.

Jason Aaron thus makes even more legible Wolverine's queerness, one in which his fighting prowess is not the predominant trait that Logan must display. He must be vulnerable and open to the students, especially Quire, who sees Wolverine as an authority figure to resist. Logan and the other teachers figure out that the school has been built on a grandchild of Krakoa who is being mind-controlled by a new teenager-led Hellfire Club. The Hellfire Club is forcing the grandchild of Krakoa to destroy the school. When the Krakoa grandchild attacks, the reader gets depictions of Wolverine hacking away at the rock as the whole school tries to figure out why the literal ground is swallowing them up. Wolverine leads the students in using their mutant powers to come together as a community of students. Logan's violence is tamped down by his worries about passing the education inspection, teaching and mentoring the students, and reforming the most troublesome of mutants, Kid Omega.

It is perhaps most evident in the art that we see Wolverine's representation most experimented on. For example, in Mark Bachalo's early rendering, Wolverine is still slightly angular, rough, hairy, and dressed professionally. Bachalo's line work emphasizes the Wolverine-ruggedness that readers of mutant comics have grown familiar. It is an ugly Wolverine. But, by the time Nick Bradshaw takes over in Issue #4, Wolverine has become softer, and his features are more rounded. Bradshaw's version is a much more aesthetically pleasing Wolverine. Nurture has transformed the usual angular and ripped body of Wolverine into a softer body, replete with comfy sweaters and coffee mugs. One of the things that Aaron's story and Bradshaw's art does in this series is bring the conflicting characteristics of Wolverine to the surface. Everyone knows the battle-hardened Wolverine, but Bradshaw's art emphasizes the much more nurturing Professor Logan.

It is also in the opening of this series that we glimpse another change for Wolverine as he mentors a young man, Quentin Quire, Kid Omega. Wolverine has always mentored female mutants: Kitty Pryde, Armor, Laura, and Jubilee. However, in this series, Wolverine mentors a young man and a very powerful mutant. In a flashback, the reader sees Wolverine take Quentin Quire off the hands of the Avengers who have arrested him for the events of *Schism* (in which Quire forces world leaders to reveal their darkest secrets on camera). Quentin resists Wolverine at every turn, even making fun of Logan's mentoring in a metafictional nod to the audience regarding Wolverine's past:

> I can't wait for that scene in the third act when your tough love finally breaks through my thorny exterior to reach the frightened, lonely little boy underneath, there won't be a dry eye in the house. Should we skip the drama and just hug it out right here?
>
> (Aaron and Bachalo, *Wolverine and the X-Men* #3, 2012)

By the end of the first arc, however Wolverine does get through to him. While other mutants fight Krakoa's grandchild, Quentin acts to communicate with him as it is attacking the school by appealing to their shared sense of loneliness and need for place and belonging in the mutant community. It is revealed that the grandchild of Krakoa really wants to be a member of the school, but is being manipulated by the Hellfire Club. The very same struggles that Wolverine has symbolized—the loner who understands what it means to not belong within the mutant world—become sign posts for Quentin. In turn, Quire uses the lessons that Wolverine has taught him to reach out to the grandchild and forge a bond. Later, when Wolverine dies (during *The Death of Wolverine* series [2014]), Quentin realizes his own potential as a member of the mutant community. Quentin Quire's story moves from rebelling teenage to member of the mutant community all while maintaining his snarky identity. As

Wolverine models, belonging in the mutant world always means being a mutant on one's own terms.

It's significant that at the end of this arc of *Wolverine and the X-Men* Wolverine is attempting to mentor a male-identified teenager. And, even more significant, that he has taken on being a headmaster for a whole school. His ability to be attentive to where the students are, and the ways in which they need individual cultivating are important to his character. Kid Omega is an omega-level mutant. The kind of enraged masculinity that Quentin exhibits is something Wolverine is familiar with. Wolverine has the opportunity to guide that anger into something more productive. Kid Omega is a young Wolverine, untested, arrogant, violent, maybe a little more self-aware, but certainly in need of nurture. Here is another way Logan seeks to model a queer masculinity; his mentoring of Kid Omega, unlike his female mentees, puts Wolverine in a position to face a version of himself. However, rather than try to kill that mirror image (as he does in the movie, *Logan*), Wolverine can use nurture, love, and kinship to model a new path forward for Kid Omega. In the end, Wolverine shows how the "lonely little boy" can become a member of the mutant community (while maintaining his own unique identity).

Wolverine and the Android

Kitty Pryde and Wolverine and *Wolverine and the X-Men* depict Wolverine as a loving mentor toward mutants who are trying to understand their path. Wolverine's expanding sense of nurture extends, however, even beyond mutants. His sense of kinship for those society does not deem human is evidenced by his relationship with the android child, Elsie Dee. Wolverine's recognition of her as a being which he cares for and nurtures, despite the attitudes around him which relegate Elsie Dee to a "thing," is yet another way the character of Wolverine queers relationships, even those of the non-human.

Elsie Dee is introduced in *Wolverine* #37 (*Essential Wolverine* Vol. 2), where she is depicted floating in a vat not dissimilar from Wolverine's own creation *via* a science lab in his *Weapon X* storyline. Donald Pierce creates her in the form of a little girl for the purpose of killing Wolverine. Donald Pierce, leader of the Reavers, long-time foes of the X-Men, and a group made up itself of cyborg killers, wants revenge for all of the damage that Wolverine has caused him and his crew. Along with an android clone of Wolverine, Albert, Elsie Dee is to entice Wolverine into an act of heroism. Once he is near her, she is to detonate herself, killing them both. Pierce has packed her with plastic explosives. Important to this plot, however, is that Bonebreaker, one of the Reavers, has uploaded her with the "maximum logic program" accidentally, as Pierce has wanted her only to have the brain patterns of a five-year-old child.

Donald Pierce is counting on Elsie Dee's appearance as a child to appeal to Wolverine's sense of heroism. His heroism, then, will prove to be his death. However, because of Elsie Dee receiving the "maximum logic program," she is able to reason that her own self-destruction can be avoided. In other words, she is aware that she is both programmed to self-destruct, but also aware that she can enact a plan of self-preservation. She needs to overwrite her programming. She enacts her plan by first upgrading Albert and decides that if Albert can defeat Wolverine, then Logan will not come near her, and she will not have to self-detonate.

Upon his own logic upgrade, Albert and Elsie Dee form a bond similar to that of Wolverine and his mentees. Albert reports to Elsie Dee that he "feels things" (*Essential Wolverine* Vol. 2) and does not want to be alone if Elsie Dee should die. Hama humanizes the androids through their own loving attachment so that they become empathetic victims in Pierce's plan. With the villain off-scene, the reader identifies with the misfit androids, sparking the reader's own sense of ethical response for the other. Although Albert tries to defeat Wolverine, he fails, meaning that Elsie Dee must fulfill her programming. In order to attract Wolverine to her rescue, she sets the warehouse she's been hiding in on fire, screaming from the window for Wolverine to save her.

Thus far this story has also contained a subplot in which the X-Woman, Storm, has been hunting for Wolverine. Storm works as the foil for affection toward the androids. If the reader and Wolverine have been taken in by an affective response toward Elsie Dee and Albert, Storm works as the voice of skepticism; she does not trust Elsie Dee. If the prevailing attitude toward robots is that they are "things," the question raised by these issues of *Wolverine* is what do humans owe androids as things? In this case, the ethical stakes are even higher, as these are robots who are sent to kill the protagonist. When Storm helps Wolverine defeat Albert, she also articulates her concern that Elsie Dee may be his accomplice (*Essential Wolverine* Vol. 2). Hearing Elsie Dee screaming for help from the window of the burning warehouse, Wolverine rushes toward the building anyway, explaining: "yeah, but I don't intend to let a real kid burn up on account of a 'could'" (*Essential Wolverine* Vol. 2).

As Elsie Dee witnesses Wolverine fighting to save her through the fire, she begins to regret her plans. As he appears before her with his flesh burning and his hair missing from the flames, she starts to feel regret. Reporting to Albert via a radio connection in their respective brains, she comments, "he's all burnt up, Albert! He's all burnt up and he still kept comin' for me ... he suffered for me and now he's going to die for me" (*Essential Wolverine* Vol. 2). Wolverine's pained and traumatized body yet again becomes the locus for relationality. Elsie Dee is inspired by the lengths of his empathetic reaction. The full-page image delivered after Elsie Dee's speech shows Wolverine holding her close, shielding her from the flames; it is an embrace of comfort in the midst of chaos. Silvestri draws billowing smoke circling around them, as well as coming from Wolverine's skin, and falling rain care of Storm's weather power—a kinetic image which emotes affection. Wolverine does not know she is an android, just that he has rushed into a burning building to save a child. In the inset panel of the full page, Elsie Dee whispers to the reader (her eyes looking out from the page at the reader): "now that somebody really cares about me, it's going to be all over" (*Essential Wolverine* Vol. 2).

As Larry Hama has built up the emotional tension for the reader by showing Elsie Dee's conflicting sense of self-preservation and duty in terms of her very programming, the test becomes how the characters will respond to Elsie Dee once she has revealed herself (or has come out). With the suspense mounting Elsie Dee comes clean, "I'm an android. I'm packed full of plastic explosives and wight now I'm using all of my concentration to override the detonation program" (*Essential Wolverine* Vol. 2). Normally, one would run from such a proclamation and Storm immediately orders Wolverine to "drop that thing and get away from it" (*Essential Wolverine* Vol. 2).

Storm's pronoun change from "she" to "it" reveals her prejudicial response to objects. And, we can't blame her—the ethical concern over what humans owe to things has a long philosophical history. How can the human relate to the android programmed for killing? Is the android a thing predetermined to obey its programming, or is it a thing capable of making choices? Is it even a thing? Storm's vote is clear: it is a thing that should be cast out. For Storm, Elsie Dee has gone from a recognizable self, a child, to a thing. Storm pleads for Wolverine to get away, "it's not a real little girl. It's a construct. A cleverly programmed puppet" (*Essential Wolverine* Vol. 2). In many ways, Storm is correct. The reader has seen Pierce construct Elsie Dee and program her. The reader knows Elsie Dee's prime directive, and yet, over the course of this arc, Hama has created a tension between the android-as-thing and the android-as-other, something that challenges the reader's sense of empathy. A reader cannot help but see that Elsie Dee's creation and manipulation mirror Wolverine's own weaponization at the hands of the Weapon X program. The reader roots for Elsie Dee knowing that she may be "not a real little girl" but still recognizing her ability for choice, and, thus, somehow "alive."

Silvestri uses an aspect-to-aspect treatment to effectively allow the reader to *see* what Wolverine is seeing. Wolverine refuses to release Elsie Dee. In a three-panel sequence, Elsie Dee pleads for him to leave her so that she can explode. However, Silvestri transitions from Elsie Dee's whole face in one panel to just the one eye of Logan in the next panel, then, following those two panels, just Elsie Dee's tear-filled eye. In this way, Silvestri shows how Wolverine does not reduce her to a "thing" or "it," rather, he views Elsie Dee with more complexity and recognizes her trauma. Even if it should mean their lives, he does not want her to suffer. Wolverine, as well, understands here that androids suffer, and it is his duty to help her in her process.

Wolverine reasons that if Elsie Dee is willing to sacrifice herself, then there is something within her that is beyond mere programming. In other words, Elsie Dee's sense of self-preservation also proves that her ability to reason can overwrite her self-destruction. For Wolverine anything that can choose, can also overcome the darkness (in this case her android suicide; in his case, the berserker). The comment is, of course, self-reflective, Wolverine himself has been called a cyborg in light of his adamantium skeleton, and a strong thread in his own story is understanding his own subjectivity, especially as he battles the "berserker" or "beast" within. The question of what it means to be human continually haunts his character. In this way, Wolverine empathizes with Elsie Dee's plight: to give in to her programming is akin to Wolverine giving in to his berserker self.

While Storm continues to chide Logan for thinking Elsie Dee is "real," Wolverine reasons with Elsie to amend her programming. Luckily, an injured Albert, made smarter by Elsie Dee, is able to upload the sequence that allows her to stall the programming. While Wolverine hugs Elsie Dee in celebration, Storm comments, "you certainly have a way with girls, Logan…girls of all ages and constructs" (Hama and Silvestri, *Wolverine* #39). Storm, through Wolverine, then, recognizes her as a girl, not just an object, but a being with subjectivity. She comes around to Wolverine's expansive sense of affective commitment. While Storm at first refuses Elsie Dee's pronouns, and reduces her to a thing, not recognizable for human attachment, Wolverine respects Elsie Dee as a self, albeit a self that is full of plastic explosives, but a being nonetheless. While the reader witnesses Elsie Dee's construction and her actions as an android, this does not take away from the reader's empathy with her. The comic book which often challenges readers to empathize with the radical other—the monster, the mutant, the android, the alien—suggests a capacious and queer sense of community. Even the android commands empathetic care (even if it is trying to destroy humanity). Wolverine's radical queer ethics, extending relations to the other, suggests an affinity—a parliament of things of which the human is part—where all humans and non-humans are worthy of affective care. Wolverine practices this affective relation to Kitty Pryde, to Quentin Quire, and to Elsie Dee, proving his own sense of a parliament of beings is founded with radical love.

Wolverine is a character that embodies hybridity—both hero and antihero, as well as, a masculine nurturer. Wolverine offers us a way forward in thinking about the superhero. Rather than emphasizing individualism in superheroics, Wolverine's characterization emphasizes the ways that care and love through kinship and broadening affiliations are key to a queer heroic futurity. Building on Wolverine's open body and his forging of queer kinship, in the next chapter I turn to the ways fanfiction communities have represented Wolverine's love and relationships, focusing on his friendship with Kurt Wagner, Nightcrawler, and the ways that fanfiction represents their relationships as kinky with erotic joy.

Notes

1 Sara Ahmed, *The Promise of Happiness* (Durham, NC: Duke University Press, 2010), see especially Chapter 3, pp. 88–120.

2 Discussions of homonormativity have also spread into comic book studies, for example, see E. De. Dauw, "Homonormativity in Marvel's *Young Avengers*: Wiccan and Hulkling's Gender Performance," *Journal of Graphic Novels and Comics* 9, no. 1 (2017): 61–74.

3 See Richard Reynold's reading of this issue in *Superheroes: A Modern Mythology* (1992) where he points out how Wolverine encourages Colossus to be a part of the X-Men team despite their different backgrounds (pp. 84–95).

4 See Chris Claremont (writer) and Frank Miller (artist), *Wolverine* (New York: Marvel, 2013).

5 For example, in Miles Body, *Marvel's Mutants: The X-Men Comics of Chris Claremont* (London: I.B Tauris, 2018) a rundown of Claremont's work on mutant comics, *Kitty Pryde and Wolverine* is mentioned only in passing and only in reference to how Wolverine deals with the villain.

6 Kitty Pryde's first appearance is in Chris Claremont and John Byrne, "God Spare the Child," *Uncanny X-Men* #129 (1980) (New York: Marvel Comics).

7 For a discussion of failure in superhero development, see Ben Saunders, *Do the Gods Wear Capes? Spirituality, Fantasy, and Superheroes* (New York: Continuum, 2011), especially Chapter 3, "Spider-Man: Heroic Failure and Spiritual Triumph" (pp. 72–103).

8 Guiding my thought in this section is the work of Jack Halberstam, especially *The Queer Art of Failure* (Durham, NC: Duke University Press, 2011) and his "Queer Betrayals," in *Queer Futures: Reconsidering Ethics, Activism, and the Political.* Eds. Elahe Haschemi Yekani, Eveline Kilian, and Beatrice Michaelis (London: Routledge, 2013). 177–190.

9 See Gerry Dugan (writer) and Mateo Lolli (artist), *Marauders* #1 (New York: Marvel, 2019).

3 Queering Wolverine in Fan Fiction

While the first two chapters of this project have worked to explore the queer bodily representations and queer relationships that writers and artists have used to shape the character of Wolverine in comics, fans have also taken the queer subtext and extended it in meaningful ways. This chapter focuses on fandom, specifically fanfiction, as it has played with Wolverine in more explicitly sexual and queer terms. In this chapter, I first examine the world of fanfiction in more general terms, exploring how it answers back to the queerbaiting found in much of corporately owned comics. Fanfiction is a space in which fans subvert subtext and bring queer representation to the surface by rewriting characters and relationships. My contention is that fanfiction authors queer Wolverine by playing with his hypermasculinity, especially in his relationship with Kurt Wagner/Nightcrawler to show that Wolverine is more sexually fluid than the comics allow which, in turn, also affects how readers approach Wolverine. This recursive relationship between fan writing and the comics themselves make the world of fanfiction and the world of comics a dynamic site for queer transformations and suggest that fanfiction vitally contributes to the discussions of queer representation in the comic world. I will first discuss the problem of queerbaiting and how it find its way into the current family of X-Men comics. I then turn to examples from fanfiction that play with the representation of Wolverine through BDSM and other kinds of romantic and sexual relationships. These examples of fanfiction add to this archive of queer Wolverine stories as they extend and add to the character's representation as a queer mutant. By playing with Logan in these stories, these writers are bringing the queer subtext to the surface and shedding a light on Wolverine's queer body and relationships in more frankly erotic terms.

Queerbaiting and Fanfiction

In 2019 Jonathan Hickman (writer) and Pepe Laraz (artist) revamped the line of X-Men comics in what is known as the *House of X/Power of X* storyline. In these stories, the mutants discovered how to cheat death, and their ambitions grew as they founded a mutant nation on the island of Krakoa and a colony on

DOI: 10.4324/9781003222644-4

Mars where only mutants were invited to live. The promise in these new stories was that the mutants were also more queer. One way this new queerness was expressed was through a diagram of the Summer's family home located on the moon. In one informational diagram (or infographic) of the living space, the readers see that Scott Summers (mutant name: Cyclops), Jean Grey (mutant name: Marvel Girl), and Logan (mutant name: Wolverine) have rooms next to each other.[1] Jean Grey's room is open to both Cyclop's and Wolverine's rooms. Fans reacted by celebrating this visual nod to Jean's, Scott's and Logan's polyamorous relationship, also teasing that Scott and Logan were now bisexual.[2] A polyamorous, bisexual relationship represented in a major comic book published by one of the big two is a huge move. In terms of Scott's and Logan's bisexuality, Maria Gurevich, Helen Bailey, and Jo Bower write,

> bisexuality unsettles—sociopolitically, psychically, and, at its core, epistemically. As an indeterminate barometer of sexual and gender referents and preferences its unsettling valences are multiple. It disturbs existing sexed and gendered categories, refusing obstinately to settle as a fixed gendered or sexed subject or upon a singular gendered or sexed object.
>
> (2012: 44)

Bisexuality's indeterminacy disrupts easy representation in comics and it is both a celebratory and intriguing move by the writer. Yet, the Logan-Scott-Jean relationship, while visually hinted at, is never out right confirmed by the creators or within the story itself. While fan speculation seemed to agree that this new *status quo* of these three characters has moved from a three-way romantic rivalry to polyamorous lovers, this "gesture-without-confirmation" is also an example of what scholar's call "queer baiting."[3]

Queer baiting has a long history in media, and fans have called out creators and producers of media for this exploitative tactic (Hale 2021). As Monique Franklin writes,

> the term 'queer baiting' has become prominent within fan discussions in recent years to describe the idea that producers of media content are deliberately placing hints that certain characters may be queer specifically to gain the interest of queer audiences with no intention to deliver this promise.
>
> (2019: 41)

While the Jean-Scott-Logan polyamorous and bisexual relationship has been taken as "canon" by fans, the creators of the X-Men have done little to confirm or deny that this relationship is in fact a new part of the mutant canon. As Jonathan Hickman said in a podcast interview:

> I like to think that we push it as far as we possibly can. I like to think that we have creators who want to tell stories that are very important to them as

creators, and I think the most that I can do—and I feel like the most that I did while I was there—was, I support them wholeheartedly.

(qtd. in Bacon 2022)

Hickman admits that there are corporate constraints as to how far they can push representation. It falls to the fan to pick up the challenge.

Queerbaiting is a problem, of course, as it does not outright confirm representation, instead remaining comfortable by hiding within subtext. Decoding subtext can be enjoyable for those communities in the know, but it also robs media, including comics, of the opportunity to represent a myriad of possibilities for representation, especially marginalized communities who only see that the overwhelming majority of characters are white, cis, male, and heterosexual. However, as Franklin also points out, by raising the cry of queerbaiting there is also the risk of a loss of ambiguity in identity that queer culture embraces:

> this … raises the question of what is counted as queer identity, which brings up current anxieties about fluidity and permeability. If an identity is not claimed, it must be sufficiently shown to be considered irrefutable and the portrayals that are contentious in this area are those that trouble binary distinctions of identity boundaries.

(2019: 45)

For Franklin, calling out queerbaiting is a double-edged sword—it is a weapon fans can use to call out producers to be more responsible in delivering on the promise of queer representation, but it can also become a blunt weapon by which the wielder insists on claiming clear identity positions despite queerness itself being fluid and open, eschewing dogmatic binaries. In the end, Franklin notes:

> None of these problems are inherent in the concept. It is possible to advocate for more explicit representation of queer identities and cultures without maintaining these identities are rigidly essential. It is possible to consider implicit representation "real" while pointing out that it should not be the only representation available, and it is likewise possible to consider audience interpretations valid while calling out producers for attempting to manipulate and then disavow these. What is inherent in the concept is the need to solve a problem—the lack of visibility and the additional problems that come with it.

(2019: 52)

Franklin advocates for the validation of audience interpretations as a force for acknowledging the queer possibilities of a text.

Karen Hellekson and Kristin Busse define fanfiction as "the imaginative interpolations and extrapolations by fans of existing literary worlds" (2014:

5–6). Fanfiction and the study of it has exploded alongside technological in-
novation.[4] Early fanfiction was published in fanzines usually aimed at a particular fandom. Now fanfiction can be found all over the internet with multiple
platforms hosting the work of fan creators. While the field of fanfiction studies
began with a focus on *Star Trek* fandom, fandom itself has exploded to en-
compass all forms of popular media, including television, comics, films, and
video games resulting in subfields within fanfiction studies. Henry Jenkins's
work, *Textual Poachers* (1992) is considered the touchstone book for the field
of fan studies. Jenkins emphasizes participatory culture and the ways fans
can shape fandom; as he writes, critiquing Michel de Certeau's concept of the
textual poacher, "poachers do not observe from the distance (be it physical,
emotional, or cognitive); they trespass upon others' property; they grab it and
hold onto it; they internalize its meaning and remake these borrowed terms"
(Jenkins 2013: 62). Jenkins's work is foundational to fan studies and is helpful in providing heuristic tools to frame the vast expanse that encompasses
fanfiction.

Building on Jenkin's *Textual Poachers,* Hellekson and Busse point out that
audience reception as it is employed in fanfiction can be thought "to engage
with the programs on multiple levels, negotiating its myriad messages and
respond with interpretations and performative responses of their own" (2014:
9). Not all fanfiction is subversive as some fanfiction is invested in deepening
canonical interpretations of the characters and mirroring the stories put out by
the corporation. For this chapter, however, I'm invested in the queer responses
to characters. If queerbaiting is a problem in corporate intellectual property,
fanfiction is a response, an aggressive reading practice that wrests control of
that property and uncovers queer layers that have been left unexplored.

Queer fanfiction encompasses everything from friendships to slash stories.
As Jenkins's points out, "slash…constitute[s] a significant genre within fan
publishing and may be fandom's most original contribution to the field of
popular literature" (Jenkins 2013: 188). The most famous and quite possibly
the first slash couple is that of *Star Trek*'s Kirk/Spock. Abbreviated as K/S,
these stories explore the romantic relationships between the two *Stark Trek*
characters. Much of the early K/S slash was written by women, and, in fact,
much of fanfiction today is still written by straight or bisexual women. Scholars have tried to answer why cis-gendered bi- or heterosexual women would
invest in writing what is essentially gay porn versions of straight characters
from science-fiction (Busse, 2017). Jenkins's response is that "slash confronts
the most repressive forms of sexual identity and provides utopian alternatives
to current configurations of gender" (Jenkins 2013: 189). In much of the slash
fiction that I examine later in this chapter "utopian alternatives" abound, allowing Wolverine and Nightcrawler a variety of sexual and gender identities
often without using labels.

The level of anonymity in fanfiction calls into questions concerns about
traditional authorship. The internet has long been studied for the space it

provides people who are exploring their sexuality and gender. Sharon Hayes and Matthew Ball writes that "fan fiction communities are a significant space in which to think and explore sexuality, gender performance, and points of resistance to the widespread social discourse relating to them" (2010: 221). Hayes's and Ball's work points out that even though slash fiction depicts male/ male sexual relations, it often leaves the question of queer identity ambiguous (2010: 236). Thus, it is important to note that slash fiction, like any kind of porn, is not necessarily subversive in terms of rewriting gender identity for canonically straight characters. What slash fiction can do, however, is open the possibilities for new queer identities and experimentation with sexuality that audiences would not see in traditional publishing formats.

Fanfiction explores many facets of Wolverine's gender and sexual identities. In many ways, and without the key words of queer theory, fanfiction authors are not only remedying the queerbaiting of corporate-owned characters, they are queering the characters themselves through exploring the "potential" of gender and sexuality as it intersects with the superhero. In many of the fanfiction stories that I survey below, writers resist providing a sexual or gender identity to Wolverine or Nightcrawler in order to explore queerness within their relationship. As Gareth Schott points out, queer theory

> provides a useful framework for both contextualizing and appreciating how the implied content of comic books is recognized and realized by fans. Queer theory is typically understood as a means of navigating the evolving terrain of both gender and sexual identity, but more broadly for articulating latent, potential, or hidden (closeted) identities and how they are brought to fruition.
>
> (2010: 21)

In the hands of fans, queering Wolverine brings to the surface his affectionate, playful side. As well, by placing him in a variety of sexual situations with Nightcrawler, fans are able to dislodge Wolverine from hypermasculine traits or play with that hypermasculinity in order to show him in a queerer light. Alexis Lothian writes that

> to look queerly at fannish temporalities is to attend to moments in which they refuse narratives of development and progress by which particular moments in media and LGBT history are seen as passing into irrelevance; reconfigure norms of gender and sexuality; and use the affective technology of fannish love to build spaces that both reproduce and subvert dominant economies.
>
> (2017: 239)

If the dominant economy in which Wolverine circulates often emphasizes his hypermasculinity and killing, "fannish love" produces a Wolverine that subverts this expectation as he loves and cares for Nightcrawler in ways that Wolverine is not traditionally depicted.

Fan authors, therefore, can extend the canonical characters into new situations, relationships, and identities. Kristina Busse argues that this kind of writing is a reading practice: "fan authors [...] commit the most aggressive form of reading [...] they become writers of that text, scribbling into the margins and taking characters, worlds, and plots for a spin" (2017: 36). When reading slash fiction, the queer subtext rises to the surface. The main text, used for inspiration, is queered in the act of "aggressive" reading practices. Fanfiction authors, then, are a unique kind of reader by taking the canon out of its context and suggesting new additions that break-up the tyranny of canon. The canon, of course, can be a deterrent for growth as can be seen in complaints about Marvel Cinematic Universe movies being unfaithful to their source material. Fanfiction bathes in the unfaithfulness of canon in order to create new worlds. Judith May Fathallal asks pointedly, "do slash writers subversively create a queer subtext in the source, by way of a resistant reading, or are they making latent what is already there?" (2017: 21). Fathallal answers that question in the conclusion of her work by pointing out that slash writers do both:

> by adding its own statements to discursive formations, undermining, contradicting, and consolidating canonical constructions, fandom can and does work to legitimate what is culturally othered, including and especially itself. Through the collision of statements from varying discourses fanfic begins to create new knowledge in fictional spaces, utilizing gaps and possibilities of canon and reality to reveal basic assumptions and the possibilities they exclude. But, by the very fact that those transformations depend on canonical sources, the legitimation becomes paradoxical.
>
> (2017: 200)

Fathallal points out how much fan authors need the canonical texts in order to create "new knowledge." This reciprocal relationship between fan and source opens up new ways of reading these characters.

Wolverine, Nightcrawler, and Ao3

This chapter focuses on the fanfiction published on the website Archive of Our Own (https://archiveofourown.org), also known as Ao3. There is a rich world of Logan and Kurt stories on the internet including websites such as LiveJournal and The Logurt Fansite (logurt.webs.com), as well as contained on FanFiction.net and Tumblr. Some of the material I discuss found on Ao3 is also published on these other websites since fanfiction authors are often part of communities that span across platforms. The Archive of Our Own site allows for tags which provide an easy way to trace certain relationships. For example, by clicking on the tag "Logan/Kurt Wagner" Ao3 delivered 467 stories (as of October 2021) that contain some element about their relationship. By clicking on "Logurt," however only 65 results return. These tags are at the whims of the author and speak more to how the authors think about the story, as much as they allow for easy search attempts for readers. Tags also indicate which main source a writer may be using. For example, fanfiction X-Men stories may be inspired by comics or the cartoons (of which there are three—*X-Men: The Animated Series, X-Men: Evolution,* and *Wolverine and the X-Men,* not to mention two anime versions), or the movies (of which there are 10, including the Wolverine movies).

While fanfiction uses canonical texts in order to explore relationships in more complex ways, the stories in Ao3 diverge in how closely they adhere to any kind of canon. In other words, some stories discuss how they are inspired by or extend specific stories, while many other stories are not worried about extending a *particular* story and are more concerned with developing the characters whether they are involved in a comic, cartoon, or movie. For example, Su_Whisterfield, the author and artist of many Kurt and Logan works on Ao3 and whom I devote a brief case study at the end of this chapter, uses the web story *X-Men Infinity: Latitude* published on the Marvel Unlimited app (available to paying members of that app) as starting points for her story "Sight for Sore Eyes."[5] The story in *X-Men Infinity: Latitude* has Wolverine on a rescue mission as A.I.M. (Advanced Idea Mechanics) scientists have kidnapped mutants and retrieved information from the S.W.O.R.D Station, the mutant-run space station that is orbiting the Earth. Su_Whisterfield chooses to tell the story from a first-person perspective. Rather than scrolling through the story as it is presented on the Marvel Unlimited app, Su_Whisterfield choses to write as if inside Logan's head as he experiences relief at rescuing the kidnapped mutants, one of which happens to be Nightcrawler.[6] Wolverine comments "The flush of relief when the pod opens and he's there, alive, awake, in one piece is better than the best beer on the planet" (2021). By taking the *X-Men Infinity* story and letting the reader into Wolverine's head, Su_Whisterfield is able to focus on the affective bond between Logan and Kurt. This lays the groundwork for other stories in this discussion as fanfiction emphasizes these queer moments in their relationships. This kind of emotional response from Wolverine is not typical in his comic book form. In fanfiction, authors can punch up the emotion as a way to explore the deep feelings that often exists as subtext in the comic. The X-Men have always lent themselves to soap opera emotions, but those emotions, when they are romantic, are often limited to heterosexual relationships. In the fanfiction world, any emotion is able to be explored for any character combination no matter the canonical version. In the next sections, I offer up close readings of select Wolverine/Nightcrawler stories in order to survey the ways in which fan authors queer Wolverine in his relationship with Nightcrawler.

Romance, Sex, BDSM

While the stories that make direct reference to the media that inspired them reveal the deep research the writers invest in their fanfiction, it is perhaps when stories are looser with their source material that more queer relationships are explored. By using the canonical characters, fanfiction authors can also "genre shift" in which they place "primary emphasis upon moments that define character relationships rather than using such moments as background or motivation for the dominant plot" (Jenkins 1992: 169). In "Wounded in Battle," for example, Kimmy665 turns a typical comic book battle scene into a bedside romance. This story opens by establishing Wolverine's and Nightcrawler's relationship: "Logan watched as his husband teleported forward towards the goal alien that was swinging its tentacles all over the place" (2021). Kimmy665 does away with backstory and picks up with Wolverine and Nightcrawler as husbands and teammates on the battlefield. As I mentioned earlier, fanfiction authors do not often resort to gender identity labels, and this is no exception. Kimmy665 is interested in Kurt and Logan relationally and never mentions how they identify. As a reader, their relationship stands as husbands, and not merely friends, offers up a new dynamic to explore. How would husbands react on the battlefield, especially if one of them should get hurt?

In "Wounded in Battle," Cyclops accidentally shoots a tentacle that is holding masonry. Having been hit by Cyclop's eye-blasts, the alien lets go of the masonry which drops on Nightcrawler wounding him. Wolverine's reaction is that he "yelled and rushed forward to his husband's aid" (2021). While the other X-Men continue to fight the tentacled intruder, Wolverine takes Nightcrawler back to the mansion to be cared for in the medical bay. One answer to the question above, then, is that their relationship as husbands supersedes that of being teammates on the X-Men. In fact, Wolverine's role as warrior on the team quickly is forgotten (what we may think as being a poor teammate, actually). But, for Kimmy665, the story is not the battle, but the care expressed by Logan.

With Logan anxiously holding Nightcrawler's hand as he receives medical care from Beast, Kimmy665 punches up the operatic tones of the X-Men comic now transferred to Kurt and Logan's marital cares. When Wolverine seems to be too overprotective, for example, Nightcrawler reassures him: "'I'm ok Logan. We both know that I've been hurt worse before.' Kurt assured his husband with a soft smile moving his tail to wrap it around one of Logan's wrists" (2021). Wolverine replies in kind: "'I know. I just don't like seeing you hurt at all,' Logan replied, moving his free hand to run through Kurt's hair, making the man purr" (2021). Kimmy665's exploration of their bedside, husbandly care touches on the couple's deep care for each other and frames Wolverine as a worrier. By representing Wolverine in this way, Kimmy665 also expands on Wolverine's usual method of communication which usually consists of clipped sentences and a grunt or two. In this story, he communicates his care in loving complete sentences and affective touch.

Referencing Nightcrawler's journey to Hell in *Amazing X-Men* Volume 2 (2014), Kimberly665 further complicates Nightcrawler's own sense of heroism as he is ready to fight no matter his injury: "'considering the fact that I've literally been to Hell before and I came back just fine, I think it's safe to say that even death can't stop me.' Kurt chuckled turning his head into Logan's hand to kiss his palm" (2012). This kind of bravado is usually reserved for Wolverine and his indestructible body and healing factor. Kimberly665 takes a soap opera convention—the bedside romance—and turns it into a queer declaration of love. While Nightcrawler is hurt, he maintains romantic agency by appealing to his comic book past. Meanwhile, Logan, who usually bears the brunt of battles, is the first to leave the battlefront for the only person who matters to him. The intriguing choice to set the couple up as husbands risks the homonormative but allows Kimberly665 to represent a love story away from superheroism. Heroics are purely secondary to the marital relationship between the two. Logan is knowledgeable of the battle, but he's much more concerned with his husband's well-being. While it can be argued that Logan is not a good teammate, this story puts pressure on whether the fight is the only story to tell for superheroes. Leaving the backdrop of the battle behind, Kimberly665 is then able to proceed with what's at stake for mutant husbands (something that has not been explored in the comics, as of yet).[7]

Unlike the comics, fanfiction can provide a space to explore sex itself with characters who do not easily fit into traditional normative configurations. Like the stories above, these fanfiction authors often write their stories from Wolverine's perspective. This authorial embodiment of Wolverine allows them to explore more fully his queer range as a character. While many fanfiction stories explore queer romance and marital relations, many of the stories under the Logan/Kurt tag use sex to explore their relationship. In fanfiction circles, this is tagged as porn without plot, or PWP. While Logan can pass as human, Nightcrawler with his blue fur and tail does not. What kinds of sex can a "furry Elf" (as Wolverine often calls Nightcrawler) and a 300 lb, metal-laced, hirsute Logan perform?

In the stories I will look at next, fanfiction writers also queer sex itself. Fanfiction writers queer normative constructs of Wolverine being the dominant partner and Nightcrawler being the passive partner within the space of BDSM. Porn can become very normative, fulfilling a teleological narrative of foreplay, insertive sex, and then money shot. Fanfiction can succumb to this routine, too, but when one of the partners is blue, furry, and be-tailed, the sex becomes a lot more creative and queer.[8] For a basic definition of BDSM (Bondage, Discipline, Domination, Submission, Sadism, and Masochism), we can turn to Steven Seidman's *The Social Construction of Sexuality:*

> Sadomasochism (S/M) involves the use of power or roles of dominance and submission for the purpose of sexual arousal. Sexual pleasure is based on exercising (sadism) or submitting to (masochism) power. S/M may involve physical acts (for example, bondage, slapping, whipping) and verbal acts (for example, orders, commands, submissive statements).
>
> (2015: 243)

BDSM is ultimately about exploring the limits of pleasure. As Michel Foucault commented in a 1982 interview "they [practitioners of S/M] are inventing new possibilities of pleasure with strange parts of their body, through the eroticization of the body. I think it's a kind of creation, a creative enterprise" (1996: 384). This creative enterprise allows for play, identity change, role reversal, pain, non-insertive (de)sexualized pleasure, as well as, the "eroticization of power, the eroticization of strategic relations" (Foucault, 1996: 387). In terms of what happens within this power game, there is no prescriptive or essentialized formula. As David M. Ortmann and Richard A. Sprott write,

> BDSM is the eroticization of power. Power is a dynamic that people often try to ignore or dismiss, but its presence is undeniable in sexuality and society. [...] Using power, manipulating power, playing with power, identifying the presence of power is not something to be afraid of.
>
> (2013: 11)

As Robin Bauer writes, BDSM is an example of "alternative intimacies" that "celebrate difference, tension, intensity, risk, excess, ecstasy, wastefulness, perversity, campy extravagance, fluidity and insanity, as well as becoming something beyond the human" (Bauer 2014: 4). BDSM, then, provides a space for fanfiction writers to explore the excesses of mutant sex, playing with the power dynamics between Wolverine and Nightcrawler. The following fanfiction stories not only utilize Wolverine and Nightcrawler's intimate friendship as found in the comics, but they queer sex as they explore how Logan and Kurt relate through BDSM.

In Wolfsheart's "Marking Territory" (2–16–2012), Kurt and Logan explore BDSM. In the Danger Room, while sparring, Kurt accidentally bites Wolverine. As Kurt sinks his fangs into Wolverine's bicep, Wolfsheart writes,

> It took a moment to register what had happened and that the coppery taste on his tongue was not from him. Just as he widened his yellow eyes, he noticed something just under the pained expression that his lover wore.
>
> (2012)

In this story, Logan is a masochist. Typically, Wolverine's pain is born of a battle and writers depict him as recovering from the pain he endures. In this story, pain is pleasure, and Wolverine likes it, especially when Nightcrawler inflicts pain. As Stephen K. Stein writes:

> numerous sexual activities fall under the rubric of BDSM, so many that it would be impossible for all—or even most—to feature in a single BDSM encounter or scene, as they are generally termed. Nonetheless, the above definitions indicate the most common practices: restraint of the bottom by

the top, infliction of pain through flagellation or other means, and a hierarchy of dominance and submission.

(2021: 2)

While Kimmy665 focused on romance and care in their marital relationship, Wolfsheart plays with what goes on within a BDSM encounter, as well as, exploring the erotics of fighting in the Danger Room (figured as a kind of BDSM dungeon). While Wolfsheart uses the set-up of the Danger Room, the X-Men's hard-light holographic training facility, the author also turns it into a site for the discovery of sexual play.

While the story moves to describing the sex scene, Wolfsheart further explores the pain scenario as Nightcrawler takes control. The assumption, because of his depiction in the comics, is that Wolverine is the dominant top in this relationship, thus their pain play comes as a surprise and delves into what other kinds of sex play these two characters could have.[9] Wolverine is "juiced up" after a fight with Cyclops, and Kurt takes advantage. Their sex play begins with Wolverine pinning Nightcrawler to the bed, assumedly as he had done many times before. Yet, in his attempt to dominate Nightcrawler, he does not foresee that Kurt is going to turn the tables. Wolfsheart uses the hypermasculine Logan as a foil to what is about to happen.

Nightcrawler teleports from beneath Logan ending up pinning Wolverine to the bed. Again, playing with the stereotype, Wolfsheart describes Logan as thinking Nightcrawler is attacking him and starts to fight back. Kurt has to snap him out of entering into a berserker rage, "I was trying something different," he says (2012). They start again, this time more consensually. Kurt engages in heavy nipple play, biting Wolverine: "there was a deep keening of pain to it, but there was also the sound from earlier in the day, the sound that told Nightcrawler that he was on the right track for giving pleasure" (2012). With the pain increasing, Nightcrawler turns to dominating Wolverine.

The scene shifts to Nightcrawler using his tail to open the condom and lube leading to a detailed description of their sex. While Kurt "thrust into Logan fervently" (2012), Kurt continues to bite and suck, piercing the skin while Wolverine howls in pain and pleasure. Nightcrawler leaves a mark on Logan's skin; considering Wolverine's healing factor, this is significantly rough play. As they finish, Nightcrawler makes one more pass at Wolverine's sensitive chest sending shivers throughout Logan's body (2012).

The assumption might be that Wolverine would be the dominant in sexual encounters, but Wolfsheart and other writers play with submission and domination, unpacking Nightcrawler's playful domination, and Wolverine's submission. While Nightcrawler is quick, lithe, and elf-like, Wolverine is heavy, earth-bound, a slab of beef. S/M is certainly an opportunity to explore sexual roles, other fanfiction authors explore Kurt's tail as a sexual organ, as well. Wolfsheart flirts with the possibility in the story just discussed, but other writers expand the concepts of mutant sex by invoking tail-fucking, suggesting how expansive the concept of sex can be.

William A. Jenkins argues that BDSM is way to bring to the surface a person's unexplored desires. This is important as

> the introspection that ideally precedes negotiation, the negotiation itself, and the actual play that follows can all enhance self-awareness because each step encourages players to pay attention to what they want, and if they will, to the reasons or impulses beneath their desires.
>
> (1992: 233)

Jenkins's insight into BDSM as a site to explore "impulses beneath their desires" is further explored in "Truckers" by AugustXRoderick (10–21–2021). In this story AugustXRoderick, uses the events of a story entitled "Road Trip" in *Nation X* #1 (2009), an anthology comic series about mutant life in the island compound of Utopia off of the coast of San Francisco. Wolverine and Nightcrawler are traveling with a truck full of goods and supplies journeying back to the mutant nation of Utopia. While the dialogue refers to this time period, AugustXRoderick is interested in exploring the fluid sexualities of Nightcrawler and Wolverine and the desire of Nightcrawler, specifically, to experiment with truck stop cruising and public sex in rest stops.

While this story does not name the practices involved as BDSM, there is strong thread of domination and submission in Kurt's desire for exhibitionism, while also representing Kurt's tail as an extension of his sexual organs. While queer theory has explored the anus as a site of erotic play that does not conform to heteronormative reproductivity,[10] it has yet to theorize the tail as a sexual organ, one which, like a phallus, has insertive capacity, but is more like an organic prosthesis capable of giving various pleasures as it can be shaped, whipped, and used like a hand. The tail, then, becomes a symbol of the capaciousness of the concept of sex. As well, hearkening back to Chapter One's discussion, these BDSM stories explore Wolverine's porous body but in the realm of *eros*.

In this story, which despite its basis in a comic story, quickly becomes PWP, Wolverine and Nightcrawler have sex in a trucker bathroom off of the highway while another man watches them from the next stall. Nightcrawler's tail comes into play:

> the man in the next stall watched in surprise as Kurt used his triangular tip of his tail as a hook, grasping the waist of Logan's pants, pulling it down, exposing the hairy, muscular Canadian glutes, adorned with dimples that marked each time he penetrated Kurt.
>
> (2021)

AugustXRoderick takes pleasure in describing Wolverine's posterior (a callback perhaps to the ass depicted so many times in *Wolverine* comics). The switch to the voyeur's point of view, allows for a surprise element to mutant sex. Kurt wanted to be watched in this story, and AugustXRoderick explores how a human voyeur might be surprised and titillated by Kurt's action. Kurt's tail is not necessarily a fetish (though it may become one for the man watching), rather it's an extension of Kurt's sexual body. At Logan's request, Nightcrawler also uses the tail to penetrate Wolverine:

> The two men rejoined in a kiss, more unbridled, deep and invasive, their tongues exploring each other's mouths, their throats crying out moans, bellowing and growls that echoed in the other's mouth. Wagner didn't want to be left behind and let Logan dominate all the action, pulling the tail out of him until the tip was the only thing penetrating the Canadian, the blue one reintroduced it with all the force that his muscles and concentration allowed.
>
> (2021)

Kurt's tail sex joins them in a perfect penetrative union. With Logan thrusting deep in Kurt, Kurt can give Logan anal pleasure with the use of his tail. The tail then becomes a new erotic engine as it is an organ that he can use for penetration and pleasure, despite not working toward ejaculation. If normative penetrative sex has one partner doing the penetrating, mutant sex embraces more polymorphous opportunities. During the sex act, all holes and members become sites of eroticism and gender identity as connected to domination/submission is blurred.

While "Truckers," explores Wolverine and Nightcrawler cruising and experimenting with public sex, in "Switching It Up" (1–9–2021) BlaCkreed4 writes a BDSM romp where Nightcrawler becomes the dominant and Wolverine the submissive along with plenty of tail sex. BlaCkreed4 establishes early on that Wolverine and Nightcrawler are "boyfriends" and their experimentation with BDSM is playful. In BDSM, play is important as it is "associated with the assuming of roles, creativity, improvisation, art, joy, fun, parallel (fantasy) worlds, suspension of consequences, regulations, and self irony" (Bauer 2014: 66). In this story BlaCkreed4 explores the joy and fun of BDSM, as they assume new roles: "Kurt was nervous, but at the same time he was excited. It was his first time being a dom for real, with an actual plan and everything" (2021). When Kurt expresses his hope that he will not disappoint Wolverine, Logan replies, "You kiddin'? You're gonna be great" (2021). It's a heartfelt way to start a story that is essentially PWP which not only depicts dominant and submissive sexual relations, but also removes Wolverine from his usual depiction of being in control. Instead, BlaCkreed4 writes him as a helpful submissive, encouraging Kurt to role play and explore his dominant side.

After establishing a safe word and having Wolverine kneel upon a "dildo stuck to the floor, already lubed up of course" (BlaCkreed4 2021), Nightcrawler blindfolds Logan. BlaCkreed4 emphasizes the care of consent and the way a dominate must also provide a safe space for the submissive in a BDSM scenario ("lubed up, of course"). In essence, Nightcrawler makes Wolverine use his senses, but also immobilizes him in a submissive position. To further emphasize his submissive status, Nightcrawler also collars Logan and attaches a leash so that he can control him physically. Wolverine, who up to this point has been quick with cocky comments, begins to melt into his submissive role.

The sex play begins with Nightcrawler drawing the leashed Wolverine into his crotch. As Wolverine begins to perform oral sex on Kurt, BlaCkreed4 writes that, "Logan always told him he loved treating his lovers like gods or goddesses in bed but never before had he so blatantly worshipped him; it really made him feel like a god, and it was amazing" (2021). With Nightcrawler, fanfiction stories often establish him as having girlfriends, but it is Logan who is his true lover, yet his sexuality is never clearly identified unless it's under the auspices of "boyfriend" or "husband" which the reader can interpret in a number of ways. The mainstream comics are too shy to ever overtly identify Wolverine's sexuality, but fanfiction is willing to play with what queerness in sex looks like without resorting to specific labels.

Nightcrawler pulls Wolverine off of his penis to kiss him, establishing that he is in control and Wolverine is now fully submissive: "it felt like Logan was melting under his touch and he loved it. When he bit on his lips, he could feel his shaky breath and hear his sigh of pleasure' (BlaCkreed4 2021). Similar to Wolfheart's story, Logan is excited at Nightcrawler's bites: "man, was he weak for bites," BlaCkreed4 writes (2021). Nightcrawler continues to enact his dominant role slowly causing Wolverine to become more and more worked up:

> "What's the problem, Mein Liebe?" Do you want more," he mocked him.
> "Yes, sir, please."
>
> (BlaCkreed4 2021)

More leather gear is brought into play as Kurt wraps a studded leather strap around Logan's penis, enacting edge play and bringing Logan near to orgasm then stopping: "Kurt intentionally moaned in his lover's ear, feeling more powerful than ever for the way the other reacted" (BlaCkreed4 2021). As the power play continues with Kurt teasing and Logan submitting, Kurt gets himself ready to ride Wolverine's erect penis. BlaCkreed4 makes an intriguing move asserting here that insertive sex is not necessarily dominant or submissive. Kurt wants anal sex even though he is the dominant in their role play. In this way BlaCkreed4 queers anal sex, too, taking away homonormative considerations from the act itself. Nightcrawler, however, commands that Wolverine is not allowed to orgasm. With the new rules of edge play in place, Kurt rides Wolverine pushing Logan further onto the dildo still inserted in his anus from the beginning of their play. Kurt reaches climax but does not allow Logan to orgasm.

After taking a breather, Kurt begins rounds two of their play. While they rest, Kurt massages Logan's sore muscles, again showing the care that goes into BDSM scenarios. When Kurt is hard again, he removes the dildo and begins to have sex with Logan:

> "Do you want more," he asked in a sensual tone.
> "Yes, sir."
> "Do you want me to fuck you?"
> Kurt encircled the other's nipples with the tip of his fingers.
> "Yes, Sir," Logan croaked.
>
> (BlaCkreed4 2021)

The second act of the story slowly moves to its climax with Nightcrawler using his tail to masturbate Wolverine as he penetrates him. Both lovers experience orgasm, but in Wolverine's case it is only after Nightcrawler permits him. After discussing how much fun the whole night had been, BlaCkreed4 writes that "they fell asleep hugging each other, their legs intertwined and their foreheads pressed together, smiling happily" (2021).

BlaCkreed4 frames this story within the bounds of Nightcrawler and Wolverine being loving boyfriends. BDSM play is carefully planned, consensual, and pleasing to both partners. While allowing orgasms to dictate the rhythm of the story, BlaCkreed4 explores how BDSM would work between these two characters. While I have touched on BDSM stories in this chapter, this story places BDSM at the front and center to highlight the ways power is used and undermines Logan's traditional representation as the dominant sexual partner—something we see in Kimmy665's "Wounded in Battle" where it's not a stretch to overlap hypermasculinity with over-protectiveness. In "Switching It Up," Wolverine slowly relinquishes control as the pleasure and pain increases. In turn, Nightcrawler's own sense of power increases with the pleasure and pain he provokes. Fanfiction, in this example, provides a scenario of role play within role play—by taking the characters out of their canonical roles, BlaCkreed4 is able to not only queer sex, but the writer is also able to play with how these characters would enact their own play within their romantic and sexual relationship.

Case Study: The Kurt/Logan Stories of Su_Whisterfield

Comics are known for their serial nature; superhero comic writers are always challenged with creating new stories for characters who have existed for decades. Fanfiction writers often return again and again to characters, exploring superheroes from different angles without the constraints of continuity. Su_Whisterfield has one of the most Kurt/Logan tags on Ao3 clocking in at 177 entries; her work includes both stories and art. In many of her stories, she engages with comics storylines. Often her work extends the comics and at other times her work invokes scenes of intimacy and love outside of already established comics stories. Almost all of the 177 entries listed under her name involve Kurt/Logan in some way even if the story is not necessarily focused on them. Su_Whisterfield explores romance and sex, intimacy and love, friendship and role play between Kurt and Logan, as she puts a voice to the characters in meaningful ways that queer both characters. This section examines a selection of Su_Whisterfield's stories, exploring the range of the Kurt/Logan relationship in one author's hands as an example of fanfiction's intimate relationship with the comics, as well as the way that fanfiction can bring out new facets of the character even if they return to the same relationship multiple times. Su_Whisterfield's Logan/Kurt stories often embody Wolverine through first-person point of view. In this way, she can explore Logan in complex terms. Her work forefronts Wolverine's queerness and, as discussed in Chapter Two, the queerness located in Logan's relationships.

In "All the Shades of Love" (10–11–21), Su_Whisterfield writes a story based on depictions of Jean, Scott, and Wolverine at Pride as depicted in Marvel's *Voices of Pride* (2021) anthology. In her notes to the story (usually attached at the end of a fanfiction story which frames the story for the reader in some way), Su_Whisterfield describes the inspiration for the story:

> I got really, really upset seeing Logan, Jean, and Scott at Pride. Not because I didn't want them there. It's great to see Marvel moving in that direction (not that I think they'll ever really go for it, sadly) representation matters. No, I was upset because Kurt wasn't there, too. Even if he's straight as a die, I would always want Kurt to be an ally.
>
> (2021)

The above authorial note celebrates Marvel's gestures toward representation in their Pride anthology, especially including this polyamorous thruple at a Pride parade (though not including any actual stories about their polyamory). As Su_Whisterfield points out, even if Marvel still has not gone "for it," i.e. has not publicly acknowledged the threesome except in queerbaiting gestures such as including them in this Pride parade scene, the author's investment in the Kurt/Logan relationship inspires a story in which Kurt seeks out Wolverine on his moon home (the story is set during the current Krakoan era of *X-Men* comics). Rather than write a story with Kurt at Pride, Su_Whisterfield funnels their grief into Kurt himself confronting Logan for leaving him behind.

Finding Logan sleeping in bed with Jean and Scott, he abruptly turns heel and leaves until Wolverine, waking up, catches Nightcrawler. The story depicts their deep bond. Told from the point of view of Logan (something Su_Whisterfield does frequently in their stories as a way to explore Wolverine's inner emotions), he comments that "this [relationship] is more intimate than sex" and, later in the story, "this relationship is closer than sex. Possibly closer than any other relationship I've ever had. I've had fekin' marriages that haven't lasted as long as this, haven't meant as much" (2021). This story does not include sex (though many others will) but is made up of a long description of comforting Nightcrawler by brushing Kurt's fur. Su_Whisterfield brings the Logan/Kurt friendship and its deep bond front and center by establishing how much Kurt means to Wolverine and celebrating touch as a cornerstone of friendship. It's a beautiful, queer moment between the two characters as Wolverine slowly brushes his fur while soothing his sadness invoking their long history and love for each other.

While "All the Shades of Love," is a loving foundation story to Su_Whisterfield's work, their fanfiction also explores sex and sexuality more deeply in many forms. In "Cold Rain (2-2-2020)," Su_Whisterfield writes a story inspired by the Esad Ribic cover of *Wolverine* #6 (2003). In this cover, Logan stares hungrily at a completely nude Nightcrawler. Brian Cronin writes that when he asked about the cover, Esad Ribic said "'And nobody at Marvel noticed!' And then he couldn't stop laughing" (Cronin 2017). The intentionally erotic cover also results in a number of fanfiction stories; as Su_Whisterfield writes in their author notes: "That cover. Oh boy. *That* cover. I think every K/L writer has to write the scene which goes with that cover. It's a rule. So I did" (2020). Su_Whisterfield uses that cover to write a scene of Logan and Nightcrawler in a seedy motel. Again, from the point of view of Wolverine, Logan comments "how dare I bring this exquisite creature in this filthy shit hole" (2020). By continually telling these stories from Logan's viewpoint, Su_Whisterfield is able to voice Logan's appreciation of Nightcrawler's body, and, in turn, comment on Wolverine's own sense of the erotic. It also serves to contrast the two characters: Wolverine is gruff, Nightcrawler is delicate. By establishing that contrast in many of their stories, Su_Whisterfield can then also explore how those contrasts feed off of one another and are reversed.

Nightcrawler's lithe, blue, furry body excites him. Logan comments that

> despite the rain, there must be twenty-five whores between here and the corner of the block, male, female everything in between. For twenty bucks, I could have any one of them in here with me. Instead, I have this guy. My friend. My best friend.
>
> (2020)

Carrying over a theme from the last story, this relationship is more than sex, though sex is what's about to happen; the setting almost demands it. However, there is that contrast again between the kind of sex offered by "whores," and whatever sex is offered with Nightcrawler. Only one kind of sex, sex with one's best friend, is fulfilling sex. While they shower together, Kurt performs oral sex on Logan, and Wolverine comments, "This is what love looks like, and I don't deserve it. Him. Except, he seems to think I do" (2020). In taking the Esad Ribic cover as set in a seedy motel, Su_Whisterfield is able to explore the *worth* of love. Two very different characters—one earth, one air—seem to be an unlikely romantic or sexual pair, yet when the sex has finished, Wolverine comments, "...in my arms is someone warm and soft, someone who can do what no whore can do at any price, someone who can bring me peace and can make me whole again" (2020). Utilizing the history of Wolverine's trauma, Su_Whisterfield then writes a story in which the sex that Nightcrawler offers is one of redemption and wholeness. Sure, there is plenty of sex to buy, but the sex within the seedy motel between two best friends is the only sex that can bring peace.

Su_Whisterfield again returns to the comics where she explores the deadly mission to blow up the Orchis Station as depicted in Jonathan Hickman's (writer) and Pepe Larraz's (artist) *House of X* #4 (2019). In Su_Whisterfield's "Matters of Trust" (2020), readers see the relationship between Nightcrawler and Wolverine from Cyclop's perspective. The mission is to travel to space where the Forge is stationed near the sun. The mutants need to destroy the Forge as the members of Orchis are trying to create a Nimrod, a mutant-killing android which is nigh on indestructible as it adapts to attacks against it. In "Matters of Trust," Wolverine objects to the inclusion of Nightcrawler on what is effectively a suicide mission. Cyclops balks at Wolverine's criticism, "Let's unpack that. He won't *let* me. Like he has any say in the matter" (2020). Cyclops knows that Wolverine objects to bringing along Nightcrawler because of a previous mission, led by Cyclops, in which Nightcrawler had died. Cyclops' inner monologue describes the effect that death had on Wolverine: "But it was difficult for Logan. Being without his Jiminy Cricket. His conscience. His best friend. Kurt. His…boy? Fuck buddy? Lover. Everyone knows. No one says anything about it" (2020). Cyclops' run through their relationship turns to questions when it comes to their sexual relationship—everyone may know, but no one knows what to call it. It's a queer relationship in that, despite everyone "knowing," Cyclops is not sure how to categorize it. What does it mean to be "best friends" and "fuck" buddies? With their relationship defying categorization, Cyclops' half of the story ends with a return to Cyclops asking Kurt to join the mission: "why the hell does Wolverine think I'd be reckless with who I choose? Bastard" (2020).

Su_Whisterfield moves to Wolverine's perspective for the next portion of the story to explore how the lovers react to a mission that means certain death. Wolverine comments, "fuckin' fucker. I know it's fuckin' stupid. But. Kurt. My. Elf" (2020). Despite the resurrection protocols in place during Hickman's authorship of the X-books (in which five mutants come together to resurrect mutants who have been killed), Wolverine still does not want to lose Kurt to another battle. Wolverine finds Nightcrawler enjoying the evening twilight. As they begin to make love, Wolverine thinks, "how could anyone put this precious, unique, fragile body in danger?" Not super-strong, not super-fast or invulnerable…but having him with us could mean the difference between us completing the mission or failing…I can't ask him not to go" (2020). As their sex continues, aided by lube derived from Krakoan flowers ("what kind of island grows its own lube?" [2020]), Wolverine describes their sex: "I move us so we're lying on the sofa and fuck him long and hard, when I come, deep inside, it's reaffirmation, a promise. Nothing will separate us again" (2020). This intimate scene foreshadows their death in the comic, though the mission is ultimately successful. Su_Whisterfield comments at the end of this story, "Yeah, we know, the Radiant One and his Half-Pint partner in crime will live to fuck another day," as a way to reassure the reader despite the grim odds of the mission (2020).

My discussion of Su_Whisterfield's Logan/Kurt stories ends with a porn story in which she explores Wolverine's senses in five chapters. Entitled "The Five Senses of James, Logan, Howlett," Su_Whisterfield uses a discussion between Nightcrawler and Wolverine from Chris Claremont's (writer) and Paul Smith's (artist) *Uncanny X-Men* #165 (1983). In this issue the X-Men are in space dealing with being infected by Brood embryos which will kill the X-Men and turn their bodies into Brood. The Brood are an alien parasitic race who conquer planets by infecting the population and killing them, replacing them with new Brood. The X-Men have attempted to stop the Brood but unsuccessfully. Wolverine comes across Nightcrawler praying, and they proceed to discuss spirituality. Wolverine insists that he "believe(s) in nothing, never have, never will. What matters is what I can see, hear, taste, smell, touch. Tangible things, physical things, reality. The rest is imagination" (Claremont and Smith 1983). Nightcrawler, believing in a higher power, thinks Logan must feel alone: "I'm sorry my friend. I never realized how utterly, inescapably alone, you must be, with nothing to hold on to but yourself." Wolverine answers, "I ain't alone, bub. I got you" (Claremont and Smith 1983). This is one of those historic moments that many readers have interpreted as subtext and have used as inspiration for their fanfiction. Wolverine does not speak as affectionately with anyone else on the team, and it is in this little bit of dialogue that readers see the complexities and depth of their relationship. Wolverine, taking up the empiricist position, only believes in what his senses confirm for him, while Nightcrawler, framed as the religious believer, is a man of faith. Su_Whisterfield uses that discussion as a way to explore their sexual relationship through Logan's senses. What he believes, the story indicates, is the Nightcrawler that only he can sense.

In Chapter One, "Vidare," Su_Whisterfield writes from the perspective of Logan and how he visually appreciates Kurt. Beginning with his blue fur; Logan comments, "to my eyes, he's beautiful" (2020), despite other people, upon seeing Kurt, classifying him as a freak. In this scene, Wolverine is watching Nightcrawler masturbates in the locker room after Kurt has been practicing in the Danger Room. Wolverine comments on his body,

> the sheen of white sweat across broad planes of his back picks out the muscles under the fur. Gorgeous back. He's not over muscled, not like some of the guys. Being an acrobat is a balancing act between the weight of the muscles and the power.

(2020)

As Nightcrawler masturbates, Wolverine watches from a distance, taking the role of the voyeur, though Kurt does not know he is there. Wolverine touches himself, too. This brief chapter invites the reader into the visual-eroticism of Nightcrawler from Logan's perspective and underscores Wolverine's own desire for Kurt's body.

Chapter Two, entitled "Audire," discusses Nightcrawler's way of talking. Wolverine comments on how chatty Kurt can be, but during sex "it's all gasps and groans and sighs" (2020). Nightcrawler is a "playboy"— Wolverine speculates about Kurt's sexuality: "wonder what he's like in the sack with one of his pretty girlfriends? … Kurt's the charmer, he talks them into bed, I know he does, so he'll talk to 'em in bed, too" (2020). Some fanfiction stories resist out right labeling, another way that fanfiction queers identity politics by refusing to place characters in clearly defined labels. Here, the reader gets a sense that Nightcrawler has "girlfriends" which does not make Logan jealous, rather he's curious as how Kurt may be different in bed with women versus men. The end of this story concludes with Kurt and Logan having sex where Logan promises to "fuck you now so damn hard, you beautiful, wicked man …" and he hopes to get Nightcrawler to be "a bit loud" (2020).

In Chapter Three, "Gustare," Su_Whisterfield explores taste, specifically for Logan, how extraordinary Kurt tastes. In this sex scene, Wolverine gives Nightcrawler a blowjob:

> takes a bit of spit to get his balls wet, take one in my mouth while I push his foreskin back, gently with my head, he's uncut, I move and kiss his shaft, he hums happily, and he tastes of salt and sweat and musk and man.
>
> (2020)

Later they kiss, and Wolverine comments "I can taste myself on his tongue. I wonder if he can taste himself on me?" (2020). Su_Whisterfield highlights their connection—taste joins them together, their mouths become sites for their open bodies to mesh.

In Chapter Four, "Olfacere," Su_Whisterfield invokes scent play. While Nightcrawler likes Logan to orgasm inside of him, Logan prefers to "come on him, on his back, over his balls, up his belly. I ain't that fussy. Just on him, so I can rub it in his fur, mark him as mine, with my scent. I want him to reek of me" (2020). "Olfacere," invokes their closeness through scent and how much Nightcrawler's particular scent is a turn on. Wolverine comments,

> he doesn't sweat like we do. He sweats like a horse, works himself into a lather. Fresh, it barely smells at all, but if ya' work him hard and he doesn't get clean right away, he gets a sweet musky odour that drives me insane.
>
> (2020)

The scent piques Wolverine's already sensitive nose to the heights of horniness. Su_Whisterfield invokes the comic's canon here—Wolverine has an especially acute sense of smell, so this chapter plays with scent play as a way to examine the erotics of their mutantness. With Logan's heightened sense of smell and Nightcrawler's animal-like pheromones, the mix for Logan is intoxicating. As Su_Whisterfield writes:

> It's damn well mouth watering and it makes me want to bury my nose in his crotch, or to bend him over and take him rough and fast, right in front of the whole team, add the smell of my come to the mix.
>
> (2020)

In the final chapter, "Tangere," Su_Whisterfield explores the hardness and softness of Nightcrawler's body through Wolverine's love of Kurt's fur: "I bury my face on the warm fur of his belly, just above the pubic mound where it's long, sweet, musky. My sweet, soft lad" (2020). Touch, like the other senses, reveals their intimacy and closeness. This story explains further their love-making. Wolverine rebuts assumptions that people think he is a rough lover: "I know folks think I just throw him down on the bed and stuff my cock up his ass. Wham bam, you know the rest" (2020). Instead, Logan describes how he touches Kurt to open him up for anal sex: "I keep eye contact as I slip a finger into him….I'm in to the knuckle now, gently curl it up, feelin' for the sweet spot" (2020). Logan feels Kurt and knows what Kurt likes. The sex is a sign of their connection: "See, I want, I need him to know he's wanted, he's needed. He's important to me, to us" (2020). As the scene shifts to their love-making, Wolverine again addresses the power of touch: "he connects me to my humanity, to reality, he grounded me in the sensual, in the sensation… He touches me in ways no one else can. He touches my soul" (2020). Su_Whisterfield returns to the Claremont discussion that opened the discussion of this piece of fanfiction. While Wolverine bases his being in his capacity for sensual knowledge, Kurt is the love that grounds his senses. Even though Logan can succumb to being over-sensual in his berserker rages, Su_Whisterfield shows how Kurt's very sensuality improves and enhances Logan's sense of himself and, in fact, gives him something to believe in.

Fanfiction provides the opportunity for the exploration of queer relationships and queerness not found in corporately owned intellectual property. Fan authors attempt to remedy the queerbaiting found in mainstream comics by imagining new queer possibilities for beloved characters. While Wolverine is traditionally depicted in heterosexual relationships, and only recently has he been part of a polyamorous trio, fanfiction authors imagine him in relationships with a number of male team members of the X-Men. As this chapter has explored, Wolverine's comic book friendship with Nightcrawler has provided the foundation for fanfiction authors to experiment with that friendship becoming a queer, romantic, and sexual relationship. By establishing that they are husbands and boyfriends or placing them within the space of BDSM play, fanfiction authors bring the subtext of Wolverine's queerness to the center of the stories. By doing this, these authors also suggest a richer world for the Wolverine, one in which his character can be loving, submissive, affectionate, and kinky. These stories posit that there is more to the Wolverine; just as Wolverine's body and relationships can be read as queer, he also has a full, queer sex life still being written about and explored.

Notes

1 See Jonathan Hickman and Francis Yu, *X-Men* #1 (New York: Marvel, 2019).
2 For a discussion of bisexual representation and erasure in media see Nikki Hayfield, *Bisexual and Pansexual Identities: Exploring and Challenging Visibility and Invalidation* (New York: Routledge, 2021), especially Chapter 5, pp. 85–102.
3 See Susan Polo, "*X-Men* #1 Might Have Solved the Longest Running Mutant Triangle," *Polygon*, October 16, 2019. https://www.polygon.com/2019/10/16/20916145/x-men-1-wolverine-cyclops-jean-grey-love-triangle-hickman
4 For a discussion of the intersection of adaptation and fanfiction and its constraints by corporations see Kyle Meikle, *Adaptations in the Franchise Era: 2001–16* (New York: Bloomsbury Academic, 2019) especially Chapter 2 "Fannish Adaptations," pp. 49–92.
5 *X-men Unlimited: Latitude* was later published as a print comic. Jonathan Hickman (writer) Declan Shalvey (artist), *X-Men Unlimited: Latitude* #1 (New York: Marvel Comics, 2022).
6 The artist for this comic issue draws hearts in Logan's eyes when he opens the pod to find Nightcrawler.
7 Recently two gay couples have come to the forefront in Marvel titles. Northstar, a mutant and one of the first characters to come out as gay in the Marvel Universe and his husband Kyle, who is a human, were married in *Astonishing X-Men* # 51 (2012). Wiccan and Hulking, two other Marvel characters whose relationship began in the pages of *Young Avengers* were married in *Avengers Empyre: Aftermath* #1 (2020).
8 For a discussion of the erotics of Nightcrawler's's tail, see Anna Peppard (@peppard_anna), "The sexual symbolism of Nightcrawler's tail …" 8/1/22. 13:07. Tweet.
9 For a discussion of terminology in BDSM, see "Charles Moser and Peggy G. Kleinplatz, "Themes of SM Expression," in *Safe, Sane, and Consensual: Contemporary Perspectives on Sadomasochism*. Eds. Darren Langdridge, C. Richards, and Meg John Barker (New York: Palgrave Macmillan, 2007). 35–54. Terms I use in this discussion include "dominant," or one who dominates in the BDSM session, "submissive," or the person submitting to the dominant. Also, "top," one who is the inserter, and "bottom" one who is the insertee. A "switch" is someone who can play both roles.
10 See, for example, Michel Foucault, "The Gay Science." Trans. Nicolae Morar and Daniel W. Smith. *Critical Inquiry* 37, no. 3 (2011): 385–403. Also João Florêncio's *Bareback Porn: Porous Masculinities, Queer Futures* (New York: Routledge, 2020) and Guy Hocquenghem, *Homosexual Desire* (Durham, NC: Duke University Press, 1993) for discussions of anality as undermining emphasis on the phallus as site of erotic pleasure.

Conclusion

Wolverine in Queer Time

Wolverine is a queer character. His body, open and displayed, vulnerable, proves to be a site for queer relationships, queer masculinity, and queer sexuality, and even, a radical ethics for the non-human. Writers and artists are unable to fully pin down the character, allowing for fans to engage in a queer relationship with Wolverine themselves. As can be seen in fanfiction stories, writers narratively embody Wolverine to explore the extent of his queerness. While Wolverine is violent, his most well-known characteristic being his claws, we see how comic book writers waiver in his capacity for violence: does he just kill or does he only use his claws to slash, killing only when there is no other option? Those claws are also a source of pain and trauma for Wolverine; that trauma, however, is continually erased as his healing factor papers over his traumatic memories. Wolverine must continually decide who he is, discovering how to live with and between the pieces of his fragmented self.

As Wolverine faces fragments of his memory, he becomes situated in a queer time.[1] As he tries to put his memories together or in stories where he revisits his past and possible futures, Wolverine does not experience life in a chronologically straight time. Elizabeth Freeman writes that the rise of the homosexual in the 19th and 20th centuries "trafficked in signs of fractured time. Its signature was interruptive archaisms; flickering signs of other historical moments and possibilities that materialized time as always already wounded" (2010: 7). Freeman's invocation of wounded time as a sign of queer time frames Wolverine's experience of time, as well. His sense of time is fragmented, jagged with revelation, and smoothed over by gaps. While Wolverine is represented in multifaceted ways, perhaps it his ultimate fate to deal with a queer time that further cements his queerness. In Freeman's words Wolverine becomes a "queer becoming-collective-across-time and even the concept of futurity itself are predicated upon injury—separations, injuries, spatial displacements, preclusions, and other negating forms of bodily experience—or traumas that precede and determine bodiliness itself that make matter into bodies" (2010: 11). In multiple stories, such as *The End: Wolverine* (Jenkins and Castellini 2019) or *X Lives/Deaths of Wolverine* (Percy, Cassara and Vicenti 2022) and even the already discussed *The Death of Wolverine* (Soule

DOI: 10.4324/9781003222644-5

and McNiven 2014), Wolverine must revisit points in his past in order to make sense (or not make sense) of his present and his possible futures. Because of his healing factor, he is often the last mutant standing, as in *Days of Future Past* published in *Uncanny X-Men* #141–142 (Claremont and Byrne 1981). Wolverine does not have tech savvy or the ability to shoot eye beams or telekinesis, he just knows how to continue searching through the queer time that trauma has caused in order to create a space and time for mutants to survive.

Even with his status as the last hero standing, pieces of Logan are always missing. In Paul Jenkins's and Claudio Castellini's *The End: Wolverine*, for example, Wolverine learns that he has an older brother, John, who is also a mutant. John, however, can remember their history and promises to help Logan remember—for a price. The series becomes a battle between brothers as John wants to blow up Las Vegas in order to create a financial crisis in the United States so that he can manipulate the North American economy in his favor as payback for the abuse of mutants. While Logan learns that he has a brother and some details about his early life, John dies in Logan's successful attempt to defuse John's atomic bomb. Logan is unable to learn more about his past. Logan even survives the story, despite this storyline being published in *The End* series of Marvel books. Wolverine, despite his age in this story, will have to continue to piece together his life. Wolverine, it would seem, does not end.

Queer time also disrupts familiar domestic tropes and the heteronormative family. One of the aspects of Wolverine that is an ongoing theme is his relationship with his own children. While Chapter Two emphasizes Wolverine's non-biological relationships as he forms queer kinships, Wolverine has significant biological family relationships, too. Superhero families walk a fine line between heteronormativity and queerness. For example, even though, as Ramzi Fawaz argues, the Fantastic Four became a queer family through "the production of chosen kinship based not on the conception of a universally shared humanity but on the mutual experience of difference *from* it, an 'inhuman' cosmopolitics" (2016: 72), eventually Reed Richard and Sue Storm had children turning the Fantastic Four into a more recognizable heteronormative family structure. As Stan Lee comments,

> In trying to be realistic, as we always did... Sue Storm and Reed Richards in *The Fantastic Four* had been married for quite a while, and I figured the most natural thing in the world would be for them to have a baby
>
> (Roy 2011: 38)

Stan Lee's nod toward the heteronormative pattern of marriage-then-baby as being "the most natural thing in the world" undoes the queerness that Fawaz celebrates in the beginnings of the Fantastic Four.

Despite the Fantastic Four succumbing to heteronormative patterns, mutants in all of their queerness and messy family trees also have children.

But, the problems of their biological family relations often inform and overlap with their chosen mutant kin. As Mary Robertson points out, "because of its significance of socialization, the family also has the most potential for inspiring radical change in society when it comes to gender and sexuality norms" (2019: 21). As discussed in Chapter Two, while Wolverine often "opts out" of his own chosen family, he still creates queer relations through the mentor/mentee bond or with the android-other.

Though Wolverine is involved in a number of heterosexual relationships and has a number of children throughout his long life, he only is able to be a biological father to a child once. Wolverine adopts Amiko who lives with him and Mariko for awhile; he rescues her from a dragon attack in Tokyo promising Amiko's dying mother that he will take care of her in *Uncanny X-Men* #181 (Claremont and Byrne 1984). This is the only child Wolverine is aware of until the other children meet him when they are grown. Wolverine has a biological son with his wife, Itsu, the mutant Akihiro (also known as Daken). Itsu is killed by the Winter Soldier and Akihiro is ripped from her dying body. Akihiro survives, though Logan thinks they both have died. As well, Wolverine's DNA, leftover from the Weapon X program, is used to create a female embryo which is carried by Dr. Sarah Kinney. The daughter of Sarah and Logan (unbeknownst to him) is born of the attempt to make a new Weapon X and is first given the code X-23. Her real name is Laura Kinney, and upon the death of Logan (in *The Death of Wolverine* [2014]), she becomes the "All-New" Wolverine. Finally, a clone of Laura is created, Gabby, who goes by the name Honey Badger (thus making Gabby a cloned daughter of Logan). While superhero families do tend to be expansive and fantastical, Wolverine's family is laced with non-normative births; even Akihiro, ripped from his murdered mother's womb, survives because of the mutant healing factor inherited from his father. Wolverine's family tree, even when it is based in biological lineage, suggests a queer relationality—the relationships never overlap with a "natural" sense of inherited relations. His family disrupts heteronormative family creation and bonds, disrupting normative time through fractured lineages and gaps in time. These familial relationships always must be renewed and remade, some successfully, some not.[2] However, like his queer mentorship, these relations unveil the capacity for a queer fatherhood as tied to queer time.

From August to September 2017, Marvel published a ten-issue anthology of single stories that put original and legacy characters in contact with one another. These stories brought together the old Captain Marvel (Mar-Vell) with the new Captain Marvel (Carol Danvers), for example, as well as Peter Parker and Mile Morales (both Spider-Man). In Tom Taylor and Ramon Rosana's installment of *Generations* (2017), X-23 (Laura Kinney) and Logan are united in Logan's past. Significantly, this comic is the only one of the ten issues that brings together characters who are biologically related. In terms of publishing continuity, this issue occurs after Wolverine has died during the events told in *The Death of Wolverine* (2014). Laura, having taken on the mantle of

Wolverine and starring in her own book, *The All-New Wolverine,* meets up with Logan in his past as he battles the group of zombie ninjas knows as the Hand. Laura is in a time period before she was born and where Logan does not even know of her yet. They battle together to save Amiko, Wolverine's adopted daughter. As it turns out, Amiko has been captured by Sabretooth who has planned to raise her as a weapon to aim at Wolverine.

As Jeffrey Brown points out, the comic book genre's "difficulty in portraying marriage ultimately reinforces the belief that love and domesticity are incompatible with hegemonic masculinity and the unrealistic fantasy of female sexuality" (Brown 2021: 79). Domesticity and love ultimately makes the superhero vulnerable to their enemies. The hegemonic masculine superhero is better off without attachments. Mutants have always resisted this construction, creating family and emotional bonds, love and queer life, despite being superheroes. Yet, this issue of *Generations* begins with such a premise— Amiko is an easy target for Sabretooth, and he plans to turn her against her own father in a cruel revenge twist.

Taylor and Rosana use the queer time of comics to return us to Claremont's run on the *Uncanny X-Men* in order to explore another side of Wolverine's complex representation, specifically, his struggles with fatherhood. More than a rescue mission, this story puts Logan in between a present daughter and a future daughter. Taylor's and Rosana's comic is situated at the point of Wolverine's history circa 1984 during Chris Claremont's run of the *Uncanny X-Men.* Wolverine, as a character, is still being fleshed-out. It is during this same time period that his relationship with Kitty is deepening. By queering time, placing present-day Laura in her father's past, she can undo his impulse to be the heteronormative superhero and suggest new ways of being. Wolverine's queerness circulates around his ability to forge bonds with young mutants and bring them to a new understanding of how they fit into the mutant universe, yet his relationship to his own children is fractious. Laura works to fix this.

Laura does not reveal that Logan is dead in her time period, nor does she reveal she is his daughter. Her reactions to seeing her father alive are equal parts snarky deflection, tough love, high action, and overwhelming emotion (she is depicted as choking up or looking away in a few panels). Once Amiko is saved and returned home at the end of the book, and Wolverine is about to depart again, Taylor digs into the emotional depths between Logan and Laura and confronts Wolverine with his parenting legacy.

When Logan makes gestures to leave, Laura convinces Logan to stay with Amiko. Accusing him of not being there for the initial kidnapping, Laura argues "I think you'd prefer to fight undead ninjas than spend time with your daughter. I think you find it easier to pull *shuriken* out of your body than to read a bedtime story" (Taylor 2017). Laura confronts Logan with his own complex characterization: his being a superhero is an easier thing than a nurturing path: love, support, presence. In other words, despite a high octane story involving ripping the heads off of undead ninjas, an explosive sequence involving a grenade in a warehouse of ammunition, and jumping out of a plane to stab Sabretooth, Laura appeals to Wolverine to rest, be happy, and be with his family. As we have seen, Wolverine can do supportive and loving, and he can do it well. One reading of this book is that Taylor is suggesting a retcon in which Laura's visit is the spark for all that happens after in terms of Logan's cultivation of nurture of the younger X-men.

Logan does realize that Laura is his daughter. He apologizes for his future self: "I'm sorry .... I can see the truth, It's not just the claws and the costume. You smell like me, and ... I haven't seen my mother's eyes in a long time" (Taylor 2017). Laura's body is bundled in queer time—both the past (his mother's eyes) and his present (smell) are embodied in her future self. The story leaves Logan's parental redemption open; however, Laura does convince him to stay with Amiko: "go back in there. Eat. Talk Read her a story" (Taylor 2017). This recommendation by a daughter for a daughter queers the parenting relationship as Laura is able to council her own father as to how to parent. He must do better, and by extension do better by her.

Laura returns to her present time while in the embrace of Logan; "Goodbye, Dad," she says as she disapparates in his arms (Taylor 2017). In the next panels, we return to Logan as narrator: "I'm never gonna be father of the year. I'm the best there is at what I do. But I can try to be better at this" (Taylor 2017). Wolverine eschews the accolades (father of the year) which would invoke a normative parenting style, rather, he admits fatherhood is a process, something that he must continue to work at.

Queerness exists in multiple ways—socially, bodily, genetically, environmentally, chronologically. With queerness existing in different configurations through time, it is also difficult to always account for it. Queerness continues to manifest in new ways; people express queerness in the face of normative constructs that are also continuing to change dependent on socio-cultural structures. Wolverine is emblematic of the inability to always account for a fragmented queerness. Normativity celebrates a wholeness, a smooth surface. Consider the myriad of self-help books peddling the myth of the whole self as a best self. In the face of that sense of "normal" selfhood, it is a queer struggle to recognize the fragmented notion of the self and the ways in which normative constructs of time and the body often refuse acknowledging the ways time does not travel in a straight line or how the body can be understood for its extension into space/time in queer ways that do not conform, should not conform, in their expression. Queerness is the ripple, even the wave.

Future Wolverine

In terms of future possibilities in readings of Wolverine, in other words, pushing this book into other times, Wolverine's struggles with who he is and the ways that his body has been transformed in his publishing histories, lend themselves to not only queer readings, but trans readings, as well. Wolverine's bodily fluidity, his claws that are phallic, yet cause him pain, as well as his masculinity which combines hypermasculinity, as well as a more progressive masculinity marked by tender nurturing and love, indicate that his body is not only a queer body, but a trans body. Jeffrey Brown, utilizing Sigmund Freud, points out that the superhero body is phallic in its power, while the secret identity of the hero represents the more vulnerable penis. The costume is what allows for the transition from vulnerable to powerful (Brown 2022). Yet, despite Wolverine's identity as a member of the X-Men replete with many costume designs, many writers, such as Barry Windsor-Smith, Larry Hama, Greg Rucka, Paul Jenkins, and Chris Claremont, chose to explore Logan away from the costume—the binary between phallic power and vulnerable penis seemingly disrupted in exploring Logan as a trans hero without a costume. One reading of this is that the costume is something he must shed in order to transition to his more fluid self. As Susan Stryker writes, transgender refers "to people who move away from the gender they were assigned at birth, people who cross over (*trans-*) the boundaries constructed by their culture to define and contain their gender" (2017: 1). Stryker further writes "it is the movement across a socially imposed boundary away from an unchosen starting place, rather than any particular destination or mode of transition" (2017: 1). Stryker's emphasis on trans as a "crossing over" of imposed boundaries leads to a reading of Wolverine in which both his (unchosen) status as a mutant and the bodily changed forced upon him through the Weapon X program set him on a journey in which he must traverse boundaries in order to discover a gender expression that might be called "Wolverine." As Brown writes, "Superhero stories also demonstrate a preoccupation with the gendered implications of the mind-body duality in ways that suggest (but not replicate) transgender experiences" (Brown 2022: 142). Although as Brown admits, gender swapping and bodily fluidity often found in superhero stories do not necessarily lead to challenges to gender binaries, as explored throughout this book, Logan does challenge easy pigeonholing in terms of body, sex, and masculinity lending his story to a trans reading.[3]

Wolverine's characterization embraces a gender anarchy that resists gender categorization. His masculinity is a vulnerable masculinity that must reckon with bodily transformation, connection to the larger mutant community, and a cross-platform queerness as fans invent and explore new queer Logans. Throughout his story, he must come to terms with his fragmented and traumatized body that constitute his queer subjectivity. Queer readings (and future trans readings) reveal Wolverine's complicated representation. My queer reading unpacks his masculinity to be layered with nurture and love. Perhaps, my argument insists, as well, that his best stories are stories that engage with his vulnerable masculinity; his queerness reveals the dynamic capacity of the comic book story. He cultivates queer kinship ties while modeling how to survive a world that hates mutants. Wolverine challenges thresholds and suggests an ethics of not just what the body is, but what it can do. His heroism is marked by his mutant powers which embrace both destruction and creation. His queer identity emblematized in his bodily fluidity, in his resistance to easy body and gender binaries, embraces a multiversal sexuality.

If collecting this queer archive says anything, it is that a more explicitly queer Wolverine is coming. As José Esteban Muñoz writes,

> queerness is that thing that lets us feel that the world is not enough, that indeed something is missing. Often, we can glimpse the worlds proposed and promised by queerness in the realm of the aesthetic. The aesthetic, especially the queer aesthetic, frequently contains blueprints and schemata of a forward-dawning futurity.
>
> (2009: 1)

This archive has looked at the queer aesthetic of comics to examine a schemata for a future Wolverine. This book was initially inspired by a moment in *House of X* #1 (2019) in which Wolverine is shown playing with a mutant child and smiling with joy—I remember being so struck by that panel, and I thought, "who is *that* Wolverine?" Seeing a Wolverine that I have never met before was a queer moment indicative of Wolverine's capacity for queer joy. More queer Wolverine(s) must be on the horizon.[4] Wolverine's story has always been in the hands of men; Jo Duffy briefly wrote Wolverine (*Wolverine* Volume 2, #25–30), and while Louise Simonson was editor of mutant comics for the vast run of Wolverine, women artists are nowhere to be found. Needless to say, queer, non-binary, trans, disabled, and BIPOC writers and artists have also not worked on Wolverine. While this book has been advocating for queer readings of Wolverine in the comics, it is in fanfiction that we can see the queerest versions of Wolverine, versions that the comics industry could be inspired by.

Wolverine's long history is tangled and messy making him a perfect candidate for my queer reading. His queerness is bound up in his too-muchness, his excess of body and love, his cowboy drag. His embrace of pain and healing is important to unpack as we consider the representation of comics and how those comics influence and are influenced by popular culture. It is important, as well, to see varieties of bodies represented in media. A queer Wolverine disrupts our thinking about him as merely a hypermasculine superhero. With his traumatic back story always in the rearview, Wolverine also promises a future joy, a new path forward for thinking about superhero energy. His both/and position indicate how this character can destroy and create. Rather than merely the Wolverine who hacks and slashes, however, it is also worth remembering his queer moments, ones in which he also nurtures and loves.

Notes

1 For a discussion of queer subtext in comic retcons, see Naja Later, "Captain America, National Narratives, and the Queer Subversion of the Retcon," in *The*

    Superhero Symbol: Media, Culture, and Politics. Eds. Liam Burke, Ian Gordon, and Angela Ndalianis (New Brunswick, NJ: Rutgers University Press, 2020). 215–239.
2 When Akihiro goes rogue, Wolverine murders him to save the students at the Jean Grey School. See Rick Remender and Phil Noto *Uncanny X-Men* no. 34 (2012). They are on better terms in recent X-titles.
3 Social media has picked up on Wolverine as a trans man. One twitter post from @ KivanBay reads "Wolverine is a canon trans man but we already knew that from his sense of fashion and the fact that so many women feel safe and unthreatened around him" (posted on 6/23/20). There are also innumerable Tumblr posts and fanfiction stories that represent Wolverine as a trans man.
4 Kara Kvaran shares my hope of more representation of queer characters in comics when she writes that "in the past decade, the big two—and some of their writers, artists, and editors—have made an effort to depict homosexual superheroes as well-rounded, flesh-out characters who are just as realistic as the next superstrong, shapeshifting half-alien" (2014: 154–155).

Bibliography

Ahmed, Sara. 2007. *Queer Phenomenology: Orientations, Objects, Others.* Durham, NC: Duke University Press.

Aaron, Jason and Mark Bacahlo. 2012. *Wolverine and the X-Men #3.* New York: Marvel.

Ahmed, Sara. 2010. *The Promise of Happiness.* Durham, NC: Duke University Press.

Alaniz, José, 2014. *Death, Disability, and the Superhero: The Silver Age and Beyond.* Jackson: University of Mississippi Press.

August, Roderick. October 21, 2021. "III. Truckers." *Archive of Our Own.* https://archiveofourown.org/works/31346168. Accessed October 26, 2021.

Avila, Mike. 2021. *Wolverine: Creating Marvel's Legendary Mutant.* San Rafael: Insight Comics.

Bacon, Thomas. January 23, 2022. "X-Men Writer Reveals Secrets of Queer Subtext & Marvel Oversight." *Screenrant.* https://screenrant.com/xmen-queer-subtext-marvel-oversight-jonathan-hickman/.

Barounis, Cynthia. 2019. *Vulnerable Constitutions: Queerness, Disability, and the Remaking of American Manhood.* Philadelphia, PA: Temple University Press.

Bauer, Robin. 2014. *Queer BDSM Intimacies: Critical Consent and Pushing Boundaries.* New York: Palgrave Macmillan.

BlaCkreed4. Published January 9, 2021. "Switching It Up." *Archive of Our Own.* https://archiveofourown.org/works/28654881. Accessed October 24, 2021.

Blume, Johanna M. ed. 2016. *Blake Little: Photographs from the Gay Rodeo.* Indianapolis, IN: Eitlejorg Museum of American Indians and Western Art.

Body, Miles. 2018. *Marvel's Mutants: The X-Men Comics of Chris Claremont.* New York: I.B. Tauris.

Bove, Brian. 2021. "'Bobby … you're gay': Marvel's Iceman, Performativity, Continuity, and Queer Visibility." 525–547. *The Routledge Companion to Gender and Sexuality in Comic Book Studies.* Ed. Frederick Luis Aldama. New York: Routledge.

Braidotti, Rosi. 2013. *The Posthuman.* Cambridge: Polity Press.

Brickell, Chris. 2019. "Saint Sebastian." 186–187. *Queer Objects.* Eds. Chris Brickell and Judith Collard. New Brunswick, NJ: Rutgers University Press.

Brown, Jeffrey A. 2001. *Black Superheroes, Milestone Comics, and Their Fans.* Jackson: University of Mississippi.

Brown, Jeffrey A. 2021. "Marriage, Domesticity and Superheroes (for Better or Worse)." 78–89. *The Routledge Companion to Gender and Sexuality in Comic Book Studies.* Ed. Frederick Lus Aldama. London: Routledge.

Brown, Jeffrey A. 2022. *Love, Sex, Gender and Superheroes.* New Brunswick, NJ: Rutgers University Press.

Bukatman, Scott. 2003. "X-Bodies: The Torment of the Mutant Superhero (1994)." 48–78. *Matters of Gravity: Special Effects and Supermen in the 20th Century.* Durham, NC: Duke University Press.

Busse, Kristina. 2017. *Framing Fan Fiction: Literary and Social Practices in Fan Fiction Communities.* Iowa City: University of Iowa Press.

Calderón, José Cartagena. 2012. "Saint Sebastian and the Cult of the Flesh: The Making of a Queer Saint in Early Modern Spain." 7–44. *Queering Iberia: Iberian Masculinities at the Margins.* Ed. Josep M. Armengol-Carrera. Masculinity Studies: 2. New York: Peter Lang Publishing Inc.

Cherry, Kittredge. January 21, 2021. "Saint Sebastian: History's First Gay Icon?" *QSpirit.* https://qspirit.net/saint-sebastian-gay-icon/.

Claremont, Chris. 2006. "Interview." 58–81. *Comics Creators on X-Men.* Ed. Tom DeFalco. London: Titan Books.

Claremont, Chris (writer) and Allen Milgrom (artist). 1984. "Lies." *Kitty Pryde and Wolverine #1.* New York: Marvel Comics.

Claremont, Chris (writer) and Allen Milgrom (artist). 1984. "Terror." *Kitty Pryde and Wolverine #2.* New York: Marvel Comics.

Claremont, Chris (writer) and Allen Milgrom (artist). 1985. "Courage." *Kitty Pryde and Wolverine #5.* New York: Marvel Comics.

Claremont, Chris (writer) and Allen Milgrom (artist). 1985. "Death." *Kitty Pryde and Wolverine #3.* New York: Marvel Comics.

Claremont, Chris (writer) and Allen Milgrom (artist). 1985. "Honor." *Kitty Pryde and Wolverine #6.* New York: Marvel Comics.

Claremont, Chris (writer) and Allen Milgrom (artist). 1985. "Rebirth." *Kitty Pryde and Wolverine #4.* New York: Marvel Comics.

Claremont, Chris, Frank Miller, and Paul Smith. 2013. *Wolverine.* New York: Marvel Comics.

Claremont, Chris, and John Byrne. 1981. *Uncanny X-Men #141-142.* New York: Marvel.

Claremont, Chris and John Byrne. 1984. *Uncanny X-Men #181.* New York: Marvel.

Claremont, Chris, and Paul Smith. 1983. *Uncanny X-Men #165.* New York: Marvel.

Cocca, Carolyn. 2017. *Superwomen: Gender, Power, and Representation.* New York: Bloomsbury.

Cronin, Brian. December 29, 2017. "Comic Legends: The Racy Wolverine Cover That Got Past Marvel Editorial." *CBR.com.* https://www.cbr.com/wolverine-racy-cover-marvel-editorial/. Accessed October 30, 2021.

Cvetkovich, Ann. 2003. *An Archive of Feelings: Trauma, Sexuality, and Lesbian Public Cultures.* Durham, NC: Duke University Press.

D'Agostino, Anthony Michael. 2018. "Flesh-to-Flesh Contact: Marvel Comics' Rogue and the Queer/Feminist Imagination." 251–281. *American Literature.* 90.2.

Darieck, Scott and Ramzi Fawaz. 2018. "Introduction: Queer About Comics." 197–220. *American Literature.* 90.2.

Darowski, Joseph J. 2014. *X-Men and the Mutant Metaphor: Race and Gender in the Comic Books.* Lanham, MD: Rowan and Littlefield.

Davis, Kristin and Kerry H. Robinson, 2013. "Reconceptualising Family: Negotiating Sexuality in a Governmental Climate of Neoliberalism." 39–53. *Contemporary Issues in Early Childhood.* 14.1.

DiPaolo, Marc. 2011. *War, Politics, and Superheroes: Ethics and Propaganda in Comics and Film.* Jefferson, NC: McFarland.

Duggan, Lisa. 2002. "The New Homonormativity: The Sexual Politics of Neoliberalism." 175–194. *Materializing Democracy: Toward a Revitalized Cultural Politics.* Eds. Russ Castronovo and Dana D. Nelson. Durham, NC: Duke University Press.

Eco, Umberto. 2007. *On Ugliness.* Trans. Alastair McEwan. New York: Rizzoli.

Edelman, Lee. 2003. *No Future: Queer Theory and the Death Drive.* Durham, NC; Duke University Press.

Essential Wolverine: Volume One. Ed. John Denning. 2009. New York: Marvel.

Essential Wolverine: Volume Two. 2001. New York: Marvel.

Essential Wolverine: Volume Three. 2001. New York: Marvel.

Essential Wolverine: Volume Four. 2006. New York: Marvel.

Essential Wolverine: Volume Five. 2008. New York: Marvel.

Essential Wolverine: Volume Six. 2012. New York: Marvel.

Essential Wolverine: Volume Seven. 2013. New York: Marvel.

Fathalla, Judith May. 2017. *Fanfiction and the Other: How Fanfic Changes Popular Culture Texts.* Amsterdam: Amsterdam University Press.

Fawaz, Ramzi. 2011. "'Where No X-Man Has Gone Before!': Mutant Superheroes and the Cultural Politics of Popular Fantasy in Postwar America." 355–388. *American Literature.* 83.2.

Fawaz, Ramzi. 2016. *The New Mutants: Superheroes and the Radical Imagination of American Comics.* New York: New York University Press.

Flegel, Monica and Judith Leggatt. 2021. *Superhero Culture Wars: Politics, Marketing, and Social Justice in Marvel Comics.* London: Bloomsbury.

Florêncio, João. 2020. *Bareback Porn, Porous Masculinities, Queer Futures: The Ethics of Becoming Pig.* London: Routledge.

Flores, Suzana E. 2018. *Untamed: The Psychology of Marvel's Wolverine.* Jefferson, NC: McFarland.

Foucault, Michel. 1990. *The History of Sexuality, Volume 1.* Trans. Robert Hurley. New York: Vintage.

Foucault, Michel. 1991. *Discipline and Punish.* Trans. Alan Sheridan. New York: Vintage.

Foucault, Michel. 1996. "Sex, Power, and the Politics of Identity." 382–390. *Foucault Live: Interviews 1961–1984.* Ed. Slyvère Lotringer. Trans. Lysa Hochroth and John Johnson. New York: Semiotext(e).

Franklin, Monique. "Queerbaiting, Queer Readings, and Heteronormative Viewing Practices." 41–52. *Queerbaiting and Fandom: Teasing Fans through Homoerotic Possibilities.* Ed. Joseph Brennan. Iowa City: University of Iowa Press, 2019.

Freeman, Elizabeth. 2010. *Time Binds: Queer Temporalities, Queer Histories.* Durham, NC: Duke University Press.

Galvan, Margaret. 2014. "From Kitty to Cat: Kitty Pryde and Phases of Feminism." The Ages of the X-Men: Essays on the Children of the Atom in Changing Times. ed. Joseph J. Darowski. Jefferson, NC: McFarland. pp 46-62.

Groth, Gary. 1996. "The Barry Windsor Smith Interview." *Comics Journal.* 190. http://www.tcj.com/the-barry-windsor-smith-interview/.

Gurevich, Maria, Helen Bailey, and Jo Bower. 2012. "Querying Theory and Politics: The Epistemic (Dis)location of Bisexuality Within Queer Theory." 43–65. *Bisexuality and Queer Theory: Intersections, Connections, and Challenges.* Eds. Jonathan Alexander and Serena Anderlini-D'Ononfrio. New York: Routledge.

Hague, Ian. 2014. *Comics and the Senses: A Multisensory Approach to Comics and Graphic Novels.* New York: Routledge.

Hale, Megan. "Queerbaiting, Marvel, and the Need for Better Representation." June 28, 2021. *ComicYears*. https://comicyears.com/pop-culture/queerbaiting-marvel/. Accessed November 18, 2021.

Hama, Larry. 2012. "Introduction" 4. *Wolverine: Weapon X.* New York: Marvel.

Hama, Larry and Marc Silvestri. 1992. *Wolverine #50.* New York: Marvel.

Hama, Larry and Val Semeiks. 1996. *Wolverine #101-#102.* New York: Marvel.

Haraway, Donna. 2000. "A Cyborg Manifesto." 291–324. *The Cybercultures Reader.* Eds. David Bell and Barbara M. Kennedy. New York: Routledge.

Harrison, Richard. 2020. "The Matter with Size." 341–361. *Supersex: Sexuality, Fantasy, and the Superhero.* Ed. Anna F. Peppard. Austin: University of Texas Press.

Hart, Lynda. 1998. *Between the Body and the Flesh: Performing Sadomasochism.* New York: Columbia University Press.

Hatfield, Charles. 2019. "Fearsome Possibilities: An Afterward." 217–224. *Uncanny Bodies: Superhero Comics and Disability.* Eds. Scott T. Smith and José Alaniz. University Park: University of Pennsylvania Press.

Hayes, Sharon and Matthew Ball. 2010. "Queering Cyberspace: Fan Fiction Communities as Spaces for Exploring and Expressing Sexuality." 219–240. *Queer Paradigms.* Ed. Burkhard Scherer. Oxford: Peter Lang.

Hayfield, Nikki. 2021. *Bisexual and Pansexual Identities: Exploring and Challenging Visibility and Invalidation.* New York: Routledge.

Hellekson, Karen and Kristina Busse. 2014. "Introduction Why a Fan Fictions Studies Reader Now?" 1–18. *The Fan Fiction Studies Reader.* Eds. Karen Hellekson and Kristina Busse. Iowa City: University of Iowa Press.

Henderson, Bruce. 2019. *Queer Studies: Beyond Boundaries.* New York: Harrington Park Press.

Henkin, William A. 2007. "Some Beneficial Aspects of Exploring Personas and Role Play in the BDSM Context." 229–240. *Safe, Sane, and Consensual: Contemporary Perspectives on Sadomasochism.* Eds. Darren Langride and Meg Barker. New York: Routledge.

Hickman, Jonathan and Leinil Yu. 2020. "Mutants are Forever." *X-Men #7.* New York: Marvel.

Howard, Yetta. 2018. *Ugly Differences: Queer Female Sexuality in the Underground.* Urbana: University of Illinois Press.

Howe, Sarah K. and Susan E. Cook, eds. 2019. *Representing Kink: Fringe Sexuality and Textuality in Literature, Digital Narrative, and Popular Culture.* Lanham, MD: Lexington.

Howe, Sean. 2012. *Marvel Comics: The Untold Story.* New York: Harper.

Jeffrey, Scott. 2016. *The Posthuman Body in Superhero Comics: Human, Superhuman, Transhuman, Post/Human.* New York: Palgrave Macmillan.

Jenkins, Henry. 1992. *Textual Poachers: Television Fans and Participatory Culture.* New York: Routledge.

Jenkins, Henry. 2013. *Textual Poachers: Television Fans and Participatory Culture.* New York: Routledge.

Jenkins, Paul and Claudio Castellini. 2019. *The End: Wolverine.* New York: Marvel.

Johnson, Brian. 2020. "Dazzler, Melodrama, and Shame: Mutant Allegory, Closeted Readers." 103–128. *Supersex: Sexuality, Fantasy, and the Superhero.* Ed. Anna F. Peppard. Austin: University of Texas Press.

Johnson, Jeffrey. 2012. *Super-History: Comic Book Superheroes and American Society, 1938-Present*. Jefferson, NC: McFarland.

Kimmy665. October 3, 2021 "Wounded in Battle." *Archive of Our Own*. https://archiveofourown.org/works/34264741. Accessed October 5, 2021.

Kobre, Michael. 2019. "Only Transform: The Monstrous Bodies of Superheroes." 149–160. *Superhero Bodies: Identity, Materiality, Transformation*. Eds. Wendy Haslem, Elizabeth MacFarlane, and Sarah Richardson. New York: Routledge.

Kripal, Jeffrey J. 2011. *Mutants and Mystics: Science Fiction, Superhero Comics, and the Paranormal*. Chicago: The University of Chicago Press.

Kvaran, Kara. 2014. "SuperGay: Depictions of Homosexuality in Mainstream Superhero Comics." 141–156. *Comics as History, Comics as Literature: Roles of the Comic Book in Scholarship, Society, and Entertainment*. Ed. Anessa Ann Babic. Madison: Farleigh Dickinson University Press.

Later, Naja. 2020. "Captain America, National Narratives, and the Queer Subversion of the Retcon." 215–239. *The Superhero Symbol: Media, Culture, and Politics*. Eds. Liam Burke, Ian Gordon, and Angela Ndalianis. New Brunswick, NJ: Rutgers University Press.

Lee, Stan and Steve Ditko. 1962. "Spider-Man." *Amazing Fantasy* #15. New York: Marvel.

Lothian, Alexis. 2017. "Sex, Utopia, and the Queer Temporalities of Fannish Love." 238–252. *Fandom: Identities and Communities in a Mediated World*. Eds. Jonathan Gray, Cornel Sandvoss, C. Lee Harrington. New York: New York University Press.

Love, Heather. 2007. *Feeling Backward: Loss and the Politics of Queer History*. Cambridge, MA: Harvard University Press.

Love, Heather. 2021. *Underdogs: Social Deviance and Queer Theory*. Chicago, IL: The University of Chicago Press.

Lund, Martin. 2020. "'Beware the Fanatic!': Jewishness, Whiteness, and Civil Rights in *X-men* (1963–1970)." 142–157. *Unstable Masks: Whiteness and American Superhero Comics*. Eds. Sean Guynes and Martin Lund. Columbus: The Ohio State University Press.

MacCormack, Patricia. 2009. "Queer Posthumanism: Cyborgs, Animals, Monsters, Perverts." 111–126. *The Ashgate Research Companion to Queer Theory*. Eds. Noreen Giffney and Michael O'Rourke. Farnham: Ashgate.

Mahn, Gerri. 2014. "Fatal Attractions: Wolverine, the Hegemonic Male and the Crisis of Masculinity in the 1990s." 116–127. *The Ages of the X-Men: Essays on the Children of the Atom in Changing Times*. Ed. Joseph J Darowski. Jefferson, NC: McFarland.

Malantino, Hil. 2019. *Queer Embodiment: Monstrosity, Medical Violence, and Intersex Experience*. Lincoln: University of Nebraska Press.

Mangels, Andy. 1988. "Out of the Closet and Into the Comics: Gays Comics: The Creations and the Creators (Part I)." 39–54. *Amazing Heroes* #143. Westlake Village, CA: Fantagraphic Books.

McFarlane, Elizabeth, Sarah Richardson, and Wendy Haslem. 2019. "Introducing the Superhero Body." 1–13. *Superhero Bodies: Identity, Materiality, Transformation*. New York: Routledge.

Meikle, Kyle. 2019. *Adaptations in the Franchise Era: 2001–16*. New York: Bloomsbury Academic.

Mills, Robert. 2005. *Suspended Animation: Pain, Pleasure, and Punishment in Medieval Culture*. London: Reaktion Books.

Monolith. "Wolverine." *UncannyXmen.net.* https://uncannyxmen.net/characters/wolverine. Accessed April 2020.

Muhall, Anne. 2020. "Queer Narrative." 142–155. *The Cambridge Companion to Queer Studies.* Ed. Siobhan Somerville. Cambridge: Cambridge University Press.

Muñoz, José Estaban. 2009. *Cruising Utopia: The Then and There of Queer Futurity.* New York: New York University Press.

Murphy Lee, "*Havok/Wolverine: Meltdown;* Queer Subtext and Nuclear Anxiety." *Medium.* May 17, 2018. https://medium.com/@murphyleigh/havok-wolverine-meltdown-queer-subtext-and-nuclear-anxiety-e1bdcd95d70d.

Norman, Christian. 2014. "Mutating Metaphors: Addressing the Limits of Biological Narratives of Sexuality." 165–177. *The Ages of the X-Men: Essays on the Children of the Atom in Changing Times.* Ed. Joseph J. Darowski. Jefferson, NC: McFarland.

Oehlert, Mark. 2000. "From Captain America to Wolverine: Cyborgs in Comic Books: Alternative Images of Cybernetic Heroes and Villains." 112–123. *The Cybercultures Reader.* Eds. David Bell and Barbara M. Kennedy. New York: Routledge.

Ortmann, David M. and Richard A. Sprott. 2013. *Sexual Outsiders; Understanding BDSM Sexualities and Communities.* Lanham, MD: Rowman and Littlefield.

Packard, Chris. 2005. *Queer Cowboys.* New York: Palgrave Macmillan.

Pak, Greg and Stephen Segovia. 2013. *Extreme X-Men Volume 1.* New York: Marvel.

Pak, Greg and Stephen Segovia. 2013. *Extreme X-Men Volume 2.* New York: Marvel.

Pak, Greg, Stephen Segovia, and Paco Diaz. 2013. *Extreme X-Men: Volume One.* New York: Marvel.

Pak, Greg, Stephen Segovia, and Raul Valdes. 2013. *Extreme X-Men: Volume Two.* New York: Marvel.

Peppard, Anna F. 2015. "Canada's Mutant Body: Nationalism and (Super)Multiculturalism in Alpha Flight vs. the X-Men." *Journal of the Fantastic in the Arts,* vol. 26, no. 2, spring, pp. 311+

Peppard, Anna F. 2020. "Presence and Absence in Theory and Practice: Locating Supersex." 1–28. *Supersex: Sexuality, Fantasy, and the Superhero.* Ed. Anna F. Peppard. Austin: University of Texas Press.

Peppard, Anna F. 2021. "'Is That a Monster between Your Legs or Are ya just Hapy to See Me?': Sex, Subjectivity, and the Superbody in the *Marvel Swimsuit Special.*" 90–105. *The Routledge Companion to Gender and Sexuality in Comic Book Studies.* Ed. Frederick Luis Aldama. New York: New York University Press.

Pidduck, Julianne. 2009. "Queer Kinship and Ambivalence Video Autoethnographies by Jean Carlomusto and Richard Fung." 441–446. *GLQ: A Journal of Lesbian and Gay Studies.* 15.3.

Polak, Kate. 2017. *Ethics in the Gutter: Empathy and Historical Fiction in Comics.* Columbus: The Ohio State University Press.

Polo, Susan. October 16, 2019. "*X-Men* #1 Might Have Solved the Longest Running Mutant Triangle." *Polygon.* https://www.polygon.com/2019/10/16/20916145/x-men-1-wolverine-cyclops-jean-grey-love-triangle-hickman.

Postema, Barbara. 2013. *Narrative Structure in Comics: Making Sense of Fragments.* Rochester, NY: RIT Press.

Puar, Jasbir K. 2007. *Terrorists Assemblages: Homonationalism in Queer Times.* Durham, NC: Duke University Press.

Rasmussen, Mary Louis. 2004. "The Problem with Coming Out." 144–150. *Theory Into Practice.* 43.2.

Reynolds, Richard. 1992. *Superheroes: A Modern Mythology*. Jackson: University of Mississippi Press.

Robertson, Mary. 2019. *Growing Up Queer: Kids and the Remaking of LGBTQ Identity*. New York: New York University Press.

Roy, Thomas. 2011. "Stan Lee's Amazing Marvel Interview!" 38–39. *Alter Ego*. Two-Morrows Publishing: Raleigh, NC, P.C. Hamerlink. 104.

Ruti, Mari. 2017. *The Ethics of Opting Out: Queer Theory's Defiant Subjects*. New York: Columbia University Press.

Saunders, Ben. 2011. *Do the Gods Wear Capes? Spirituality, Fantasy, and Superheroes*. New York: Continuum.

Schott, Gareth. 2010. "From Fan Appropriation to Industry Re-appropriation: The Sexual Identity of Comic Superheroes." 17–29. *Journal of Graphic Novels and Comics*, 1.1.

Sedgwick, Eve Kosofsky. 1993. "How to Bring Your Kids Up Gay: The War on Effeminate Boys." 154–164. *Tendencies*. Durham, NC: Duke University Press.

Seidel, Steven. 2015. *The Social Construction of Sex*. 3rd ed. New York: Norton.

Shyminsky, Neil. 2006. "Mutant Readers, Reading Mutants: Appropriation, Assimilation, and the X-Men." 387–405. *International Journal of Comic Art*. 8.2.

Singer, Marc. 2018. *Breaking the Frames: Populism and Prestige in Comics Studies*. Austin: University of Texas Press.

Stein, Stephen K. 2021. *Sadomasochism and the BDSM Community in the United States: Kinky People Unite*. New York: Routledge.

Starr, Charlie. 2005. "'The Best There Is … Isn't Very Nice': Complex Dualities in Wolverine." 65–78. *The Unauthorized X-Men: SF and Comic Writers on Mutants, Prejudice, and Adamantium*. Ed. Len Wein with Leah Wilson. Dallas, TX: Benbella Books.

Stryker, Susan. 2017. *Transgender History: The Roots of Today's Revolution*. 2nd ed. New York: Seal Press.

Simonson Walter, Louise Simonson, John J. Muth, and Kent Williams. 1988. *Havok and Wolverine: Meltdown* #1. New York: Marvel.

Soule, Charles and Steve McNiven. 2014. *Death of Wolverine* #1. New York: Marvel Comics.

Soule, Charles and Steve McNiven. 2014. *Death of Wolverine* #2, New York: Marvel Comics.

Soule, Charles and Steve McNiven. 2014. *Death of Wolverine* #3, New York: Marvel Comics.

Soule, Charles and Steve McNiven. *Death of Wolverine* #4, New York: Marvel Comics.

Stewart, Brenton. Feb. 27, 2020. "Scott, Jean & Wolverine: The Poly X-Men Relationship May Have a Queer Twist." *CBR*. https://www.cbr.com/scott-jean-wolverine-poly-x-men-relationship-queer-twist.

Su_Whisterfield. January 6, 2020. "The Five Senses of James Logan Howlett." *Archive of Our Own* https://archiveofourown.org/works/22215586. Accessed October 22, 2021.

Su_Whisterfield. January 25, 2020. "Matters of Trust." *Archive of Our Own*. https://archiveofourown.org/works/22407907. Accessed October 22, 2021.

Su_Whisterfield. February 2, 2021. "Cold Rain." *Archive of Our Own*. https://archiveofourown.org/works/22534405. Accessed October 22, 2021.

Su_Whisterfield. September 14, 2021. "Sight for Sore Eyes." *Archive of Our Own.* https://archiveofourown.org/works/33877681/chapters/84230872. Accessed. October 5, 2021.

Su_Whisterfield. October 11, 2021. "All the Shades of Love." *Archive of Our Own.* https://archiveofourown.org/works/34437427. Accessed August 18, 2022.

Szép, Ester. 2020. *Comics and the Body: Drawing, Reading, and Vulnerability.* Columbus: The Ohio State University Press.

Taylor, Tom and Ramon Rosana. 2017. *Generations: Wolverines.* New York: Marvel.

Warner, Michael. 1999. *The Trouble with Normal: Sex Politics, and the Ethics of Queer Life.* Cambridge, MA: Harvard University Press.

Wein, Len and John Cockrum. 1975. "Second Genesis." *Giant Sized X-Men* #1. New York: Marvel Comics.

Windsor-Smith, Barry. 1991. *Marvel Comics Presents* #84. "Weapon X: Chapter 11." New York: Marvel Comics.

Windsor-Smith, Barry. 2012. *Weapon X.* New York: Marvel Comics.

Wolfsheart. February 16, 2021. "Marking Territory." *Archive of Our Own.* https://archiveofourown.org/works/341533. Accessed October 6, 2021.

Wolk, Douglas. 2021 *All the Marvels: A Journey to the Ends of the Biggest Story Ever Told.* New York: Penguin Press.

Wolverine by Greg Rucka: The Ultimate Collection. 2011. New York: Marvel.

Wolverine by Daniel Way: The Complete Collection, Volume One. 2017. New York: Marvel.

Wolverine by Daniel Way: The Complete Collection, Volume Two. 2017. New York: Marvel.

Wolverine by Daniel Way: The Complete Collection, Volume Three. 2017. New York: Marvel.

Wolverine Encyclopedia: Volume One. 1996. New York: Marvel.

Wolverine Encyclopedia: Volume Two. 1996. New York: Marvel.

Zanari, Vivian. 2003. "Mutant Mutandis: The X-Men's Wolverine and the Construction of Canada." 53–67. *Culture and the State: Nationalisms.* Eds. James Gifford and Gabrielle Zezulka-Mailloux. Edmonton: CRC Humanities Studies.

Zaragoza, Alex. March 3, 2020. "Wolverine Might Be a Sexually Fluid Mutant in a Throuple—Deal with It." *Vice.* https://www.vice.com/en_us/article/akw4pj/wolverine-might-be-a-sexually-fluid-mutant-in-a-throupledeal-with-it.

Zullo, Valentino L. 2020. "Queer Comics Queering Continuity: *The Unstoppable Wasp* and the Fight for a Queer Future." 48–60. *More Critical Approaches to Comics: Theories and Methods.* Eds. Matthew J. Brown, Randy Duncan, and Matthew J. Smith. New York: Routledge.

Index

Note: Page numbers followed by "n" denote endnotes.